*Also by Susanna Moore*

FICTION

*My Old Sweetheart*

*The Whiteness of Bones*

*Sleeping Beauties*

*In the Cut*

*One Last Look*

*The Big Girls*

*The Life of Objects*


NONFICTION

*I Myself Have Seen It: The Myth of Hawai'i*

*Paradise of the Pacific: Approaching Hawaii*

# MISS ALUMINUM

Farrar, Straus and Giroux

NEW YORK

# MISS ALUMINUM

A Memoir

# SUSANNA MOORE

Farrar, Straus and Giroux
120 Broadway, New York 10271

Printed in the United States of America
First edition, 2020

Owing to limitations of space, illustration credits can be found on
page 275.

Library of Congress Cataloging-in-Publication Data
Names: Moore, Susanna, author.
Title: Miss aluminum : a memoir / Susanna Moore.
Description: First edition. | New York : Farrar, Straus and Giroux,
    2020.
Identifiers: LCCN 2019046741 | ISBN 9780374279714
    (hardcover)
Subjects: LCSH: Moore, Susanna. | Moore, Susanna—
    Friends and associates. | Authors, American—Biography. |
    Celebrities—California—Los Angeles—Biography.
Classification: LCC PS3563.O667 Z46 2020 | DDC
    813/.54—dc23
LC record available at https://lccn.loc.gov/2019046741

Designed by Songhee Kim

Our books may be purchased in bulk for promotional,
educational, or business use. Please contact your local
bookseller or the Macmillan Corporate and Premium Sales
Department at 1-800-221-7945, extension 5442, or by e-mail at
MacmillanSpecialMarkets@macmillan.com.

www.fsgbooks.com
www.twitter.com/fsgbooks • www.facebook.com/fsgbooks

10   9   8   7   6   5   4   3   2   1

# MISS ALUMINUM

I took nothing with me when I left. No photographs, no books, no souvenirs of childhood. Dressed by my stepmother in hand-me-downs, and oversized dresses from a thrift store, clothes that I vowed never to wear again, I arrived in Philadelphia in the summer of 1963 without a suitcase. My father and stepmother had been so eager to be rid of me, the potentially incendiary leader of a harmless gang of disconsolate children, that I was sent to my maternal grandmother, Mae Shields, the day after I graduated from Punahou, where I had been at school since I was a small child. I was seventeen years old.

My grandmother lived with her unmarried daughter,

my Aunt Mary, in a working-class neighborhood in North Philadelphia called Germantown, inhabited by first- and second-generation Polish, German, and Irish families, in the same small battered house where, as a young widow, she had raised her five children. In the front room, sitting on a rusty radiator, was a chipped plaster statue, two feet high, of the Infant of Prague, for whom she had made a billowing red faille cape with a high, stiff collar, stuffing the interior of his gold-plated crown with the same material, and two brocade gowns, a white one for Holy Days and a cream-colored one for days less sanctified, each with lace collar and cuffs.

In addition, there was a console with a television and a radio, my grandmother's chair, a few rickety tables with yellowing crocheted runners, and a sofa. The wall telephone was in the kitchen, which always smelled faintly of gas. I was given a small bedroom on the second floor, overlooking a neglected yard. We shared a bathroom that smelled of cigarettes and starch, as my aunt used the tub to wash her nurse's uniform. A large rusty fan was wedged into my grandmother's bedroom window to cool the house in summer.

My grandmother and her younger sister had immigrated to Philadelphia in 1910, when Mae was nineteen years old. She considered her undeserving self to have been especially favored by the Virgin, whom she thanked every day of her life, as she had soon found work as a housemaid and seamstress for a rich family in Chestnut Hill. My grandfather, Dennis Shields, was chauffeur to the same family, and in the photograph that my grandmother kept next to her chair for fifty years, he wears a peaked cap, a high-necked gray wool tunic, jodhpurs, and polished black boots. He died during the Depression, perhaps from the effects of gas suffered in the First World War, in which he served as an ambulance driver in the Army of the United States, earning a citation for conspicuous bravery under fire.

My mother, whose name was Anne, liked to say that Mae had been a lady's maid, a position that demanded more refinement than was customarily found in a house servant. She was eight years old when her father died, and claimed that after his death, she and her younger brother and sisters were each given only an orange on Christmas morning. When she was eighteen, thanks to the intercession of the Infant of Prague, she received a navy gabardine suit and a gray tulle evening gown, hand-me-downs from Mae's Chestnut Hill employer, which allowed her for the first time to imagine that she might one day create herself anew.

Clothes, which provided the means both to conceal and to display herself, became objects of fetishistic importance to my mother. It was, after all, the well-made suits and evening dresses, tailored to fit her, as well as my grandmother's insistence that her daughters learn Main Line manners and customs, that had, with some sleight of hand, transformed my mother from a shanty Irish girl into a beautifully dressed and well-behaved debutante. This is not to suggest that my grandmother and my mother had a calculated and well-thought-out plot to facilitate my mother's escape from Germantown, but rather that they knew, at least my grandmother knew, to make the most of what they had been given.

My mother, Anne Shields, in nursing school,
Philadelphia, 1941

My father, an intern in medical school, had grown so enam-
ored of the lovely student nurse who was to become my mother
that when he at last learned that she was not a girl from the
Main Line, it was too late. By the time I was a child, she had
become the woman she wished to be, and was no longer playing

My father, Richard Dixon Moore,
Philadelphia, 1944

a part, only now and then hiding behind an unfortunate and even unnecessary lie, as when I heard her gaily tell a neighbor that she had attended Bryn Mawr, causing the woman to ask in delighted kinship, "Oh, my dear, did we know one another? Who are your people?"

My mother was ashamed of her impoverished Irish Catholic childhood, and the story of the Christmas orange and other childhood sorrows were told to me in a whisper. As she was given to exaggeration, I did not always believe her, suspecting, too, that I was not always meant to believe her. As a bride, she had been treated badly by my father's family, the descendants of Quaker farmers and wheelwrights and millers, acquisitive and narrow-minded, who had come to America in 1633 with William Penn, settling west of Philadelphia in Chester County. Over time, they had lost their thousands of acres at Chadds Ford and Newtown Square, as well as their austere religious practices. They had as dissenters so proudly answered only to themselves that they had lost the gift of tolerance, considering themselves superior to those whose suffering appeared less sublime in origin; fleeing tyranny, they did not hesitate to practice it themselves. In the eighteenth century, some of my ancestors had been expelled from Quaker meeting houses for marrying Protestants and, even more damning, the occasional Irish indentured servant. One of them, a blacksmith, was disowned for shoeing a war horse. It had been as impossible for my mother, given her experience of poverty and humiliation, to feel kinship with my father's family as it had been for them to embrace a girl who, being Irish and Catholic, was assumed to be dishonest, dirty, and ignorant. My mother, at least in the beginning, was occasionally dishonest, but she was never dirty.

———

My aunt Mary Shields covered in leis. She came to look after
us when our mother died. My sister Tina is missing from the
photograph, Honolulu, 1958

WHEN I WAS twelve years old, my mother, then thirty-five years old, died in her sleep. My Aunt Mary immediately took leave of her job as head nurse in the emergency room of Pennsylvania Hospital and made the long trip to Honolulu.

My aunt was tall and slender. Her black hair, already turning gray, was kept in a neat bob that reached her chin. As she was from that mysterious place called the mainland, she wore short white kid gloves to Mass on Sunday. She used a dusting powder from Elizabeth Arden called "Blue Grass." There was a prancing horse on the lid of its round box, and its scent mingled with the strong smell of her Chesterfield cigarettes. My mother had been spirited and funny, even mischievous, and I was surprised to discover that despite my aunt's appreciation of wit, she was a bit prudish. She would turn away when I changed my clothes in her presence, which was fine with me, but not a gesture to which I was accustomed. I noticed, too, that she was a wary and fretful driver, refusing to make a left-hand turn in an intersection, a habit that added fifteen minutes to any drive, and which lasted for all of the years that I knew her.

There was immediate tension between my aunt and my father, evident in her expression when he appeared to take things too lightly, and in his refusal to acknowledge her disapproval. Her role as caretaker to her dead sister's children was not clearly defined and must have at times caused her to feel like a servant, a role that held a certain shame, given her mother's former employment. My aunt's displeasure increased when my father soon began to behave as if he were a bachelor, content to leave his five children, the youngest only two years old, in her dutiful care. He went out to dinner most nights and sometimes returned late, which naturally offended my aunt, who, like me, must have been listening for him. His name was Richard Dixon Moore, a radiologist, forty years old, good-looking and charming, with the distinction and social position then conferred on doctors in small cities and towns. I knew that my father was fond of women, and his recent bereavement did not appear to have lessened his interest. That he had many children at home seemed not to bother anyone but Mary. A neighbor once hinted that my aunt was jealous, but my aunt was so unlike my father, who was pleasure-loving and weak, that even as a child I understood that something as seemingly simple as friendship between them was impossible. It is also likely she blamed him for my mother's death.

He would sometimes take me to the Royal Hawaiian Hotel on a Sunday night. I would order decorously, a little shyly, even when he encouraged me to try things unknown to me like chicken Kiev or peach melba. His own eating fascinated me. It seemed to me very old-fashioned, habits perhaps inherited from his Quaker ancestors—radishes with butter, cheddar cheese on apple pie, salt on cantaloupe.

In anticipation of these evenings, I found a tube of Tangee lipstick at Woolworth, soft orange wax in a flimsy metal tube, which I wore for a dinner concert given by the Kingston Trio at the Royal Hawaiian. It had a very cheap, sweet smell and I don't know how my elegant father tolerated it, but he never said a word, certainly not the compliment I hoped I would receive. I wore one of my full-skirted, tight-waisted Lanz dresses, with a stiff crinoline that scratched pleasantly against my legs. My father's attention, which had been amiable but distracted before my mother's death, could not have come at a more precarious moment in my life, but I did not know that. There I was in my lovely dress, happy in my prettiness and eager to please my father, yet all the while thinking in a vague, flitting way, Be careful, don't like this too much. You are here because your mother is dead.

After one of our Sunday night suppers at the Royal Hawaiian, my father gave me my mother's pearls, and an amethyst ring, large and rectangular, set in gold, known, rather glamorously I thought, as a cocktail ring, with the admonition that I was not to wear it or the necklace until I was older. I once wore the pearls to bed, but I was so afraid that the strands would break that I couldn't sleep, and I never did it again. I was able to wear the ring on my middle finger if I wrapped a Band-Aid around the back of it, but only in my room and at night, my hand heavy with the weight of it. The necklace and the ring were my only souvenirs of my mother, other than a shoebox of photographs that I had taken from my father's desk and kept hidden under my bed. One day, however, as I left the house, I pushed the ring onto my finger, and then my hand into a pocket of my shorts so that no one would see it. I walked the mile to the bus stop at Lunalilo Home Road where Mr. Silva, the bus driver, stopped for me. We traveled past Kuli'ou'ou and Niu Valley and 'Āina Haina before Mr. Silva handed me my paper transfer and I boarded the bus waiting at the roundabout at Star of the Sea church for the rest of the trip, through Kāhala, past Diamond Head and Kapi'olani Park into Waikiki. The ride was a pleasant one, the bus plump and jolly like a bus in a cartoon, with open windows and leather seats. My hand was no longer in my pocket, but rested, somewhat awkwardly, wherever I thought someone might notice it, and admire it.

I left the bus at Kalākaua Avenue and crossed the street to the Outrigger Canoe Club for my weekly surfing lesson with the beach boy, Rabbit Kekai. I changed into my new white sharkskin two-piece bathing suit and went to meet Rabbit. As I was afraid that I would lose the ring in the water, I asked the man on duty at Beach Services if I could leave it with him. He handed me one of the small brown envelopes people used to hold their keys and money and wrist watches when they were on the beach, and I put the ring inside the envelope and sealed it and wrote my name on it.

Rabbit was waiting for me in the water, holding his long wood board with one hand to keep it from floating away. I lay at the front of the board on my stomach, my legs spread, my toes trailing in the water. Rabbit pushed off and slid onto the board behind me, his head just above my bottom, the customary position for students and their teachers. We paddled to the breaking surf, which was rarely very big at Waikiki, and he caught a wave easily, getting to his feet and then lifting me under my arms so that I stood in front of him on the board, seldom falling, until we came to the end of the little wave, when we would again assume our positions and paddle to the break.

After my lesson, I went to Beach Services to collect my envelope. The beach boy looked in the drawers of the desk, and ran his hand across the cubbies in the shelf behind him, where there were a few envelopes, but nothing with my name on it.

He shook his head and asked some of the other beach boys if they had seen it, but none of them could remember such an envelope. I looked for Rabbit, but he was no longer on the beach. I asked the man to look once again, and he made a quick search among the furled umbrellas and a pile of used beach towels, lest it had been dropped there, but there was nothing.

I walked to the locker room and vomited into a waste bin. This is the end, I thought to myself. I considered for a moment running away from home. I pulled on my shorts and T-shirt and walked barefoot to the bus stop in front of the club, my wet bathing suit dampening my clothes. Not only had I disobeyed my father, I had lost my mother's ring. I could not tell him, and I could not tell my aunt, who disapproved of my father's gift to me. As I handed the bus driver my ticket, I said, "I lost my mother's ring," but he did not answer me, only nodded and closed the door behind me with a whoosh.

That night and for many nights, I slept with the pearls in their black velvet bag clutched in my hand. I no longer went to the Outrigger. I prayed that my father would forget about the ring and that my shame would remain a secret. Then one afternoon, he asked to see the ring. He thought it could be made smaller with a ring guard. For a moment, I stopped breathing. He asked if something was wrong, and I covered my face with my hands. When he asked again, I told him that I had lost the ring. I had not yet allowed myself to believe that the beach boys, men whom I not only trusted but admired, had stolen it. My father was very angry. To my relief, he did not ask how I had lost it. I hadn't lied, and yet I hadn't told the truth, either. "I will never give you another piece of jewelry," he said. And he never did.

Although I had begun to notice a certain sourness in my

A photograph from the *Star-Bulletin* newspaper, with Koko Head
visible through the window, Honolulu, 1959

aunt's treatment of me, I attributed it to her occasional moodi-
ness. But one day, unable to restrain herself after my father took
me to dinner at Lau Yee Chai, a fashionable Chinese restaurant in Waikiki, she told me that it was a mortal sin for a father

to date his own twelve-year-old daughter. I was shocked, and the following Sunday, I told him that I had too much homework to go to dinner with him. He was disappointed not to have my company, he said, but if he was aware that he had committed a mortal sin, he did not show it.

My father soon married a woman of means from Stockton, California. Her name was Catherine Lloyd, but she was called Pat. Her late husband, who had grown up in Hawai'i, had left her several parcels of valuable land, one of them in Waikiki. We children had not met her before their marriage, which was in San Francisco, and were introduced to her a few days later when we learned the news from our aunt. Pat was thirty-one years old, handsome in a masculine way, with short hair, protruding eyes, and a yellow complexion. My aunt spent a few minutes with her before she excused herself and went to pack her suitcase.

Soon after Mary left Honolulu, our new stepmother, who had a four-year-old adopted daughter, did not hesitate to let us know that she despised us.

I FELL ILL a few days after I arrived at my grandmother's house in Germantown, and spent a week in Pennsylvania Hospital with pneumonia brought on, my grandmother believed, perhaps rightly, by shock and neglect, and which served to confirm her fear that my brothers and sisters were dying, too. Because of my aunt's connection with the hospital, I was treated very well. There was a television mounted high on the wall of my private room, and it was there that I first discovered Johnny Carson, the likes of whom I had not known existed.

Our stepmother had not allowed us to watch television except on weekends, and never late at night, and Johnny Carson came as an intensely pleasurable, even erotic surprise. The days were very long in the hospital and I counted the hours until it was time for Johnny. I would watch the entire show, distracted by erotic longing, delaying the moment when I would turn out the light to sleep, when my head would be filled with thoughts of my brothers and sisters. I would lie awake, filled with worry, fearful for their well-being and even safety. I missed the forest at Tantalus and I missed the ocean. I missed my mother.

My aunt told me that she had read in the newspaper that my father and stepmother were in Philadelphia for a conference, as my father was the American Medical Association delegate from Hawai'i. She found him at their hotel and telephoned to tell him that I was sick, but he did not come to see me. She was very upset by this, but I was so accustomed to his negligence and my stepmother's cruelty that I was embarrassed for him, and for a moment almost defended him.

My grandmother and aunt had little money to spare, and I knew that I would have to find a job, an idea that was appealing to me, as it signified independence and even maturity. The thought that I might make things hard for them was distressing. My father had not given me any money when I left Hawai'i, and had not since troubled himself to send money to my grandmother. Two years later, my brother Rick wrote to tell me that he and our fifteen-year-old sister, Tina, had run away and had been taken in by a kindly neighborhood spinster named Frieda Brown, who lived with her aged mother in a house on the beach a half mile from our house at Portlock. They, too, were without sustenance, other than that provided by the loving Frieda, who fed them Le Sueur peas and creamed chicken on toast and got them to school each morning, and even found them a little pocket money.

When I came home from the hospital, my grandmother took me on the Germantown Avenue trolley to Rowell's department store, where she used some of her monthly pension to buy me a Jonathan Logan dress, a wool plaid kilt with a big kilt pin, two white blouses, some sensible underwear, including a girdle that extended from my waist to my knees, two Barbizon nightgowns, a pair of navy blue Capezio flats, and a navy tweed Peck & Peck coat, which suggested she believed I would at least live with her through the winter.

My aunt felt obliged to listen each Saturday afternoon to the broadcast from the Metropolitan Opera House in New York, and together we struggled through a melancholy few hours of *Carmen* or *Tosca*, the living room full of cigarette smoke, rendering it impossible for me ever again to listen to opera on a Saturday. She cooked dinner for the three of us each night when she came home from work, exhausted and a little irritable. I would offer to help, but she preferred to do it herself. After a day of giving orders, often under great stress, she did not want to bother with me. As she was both efficient and good at simplifying things, she had established a menu that never varied. The first night we would have a small roast that I had picked up earlier from Mr. Miklosi, the butcher at the end of the street, a package of frozen French-cut string beans, and a baked potato with large amounts of butter, salt and pepper, and sour cream. The second night we would have what was left of the cold roast beef, string beans, and a potato. The third night, when the meat was finished, we had scrambled eggs and canned tomatoes. It was all delicious, especially as my brothers and sisters and I had barely survived on the scant portions of lukewarm powdered milk, powdered mashed potatoes, and SpaghettiOs allowed us by our stepmother. I especially loved what I came to think of as Egg Night. Occasionally, there would be a special treat of Sara Lee cheesecake. My aunt kept a raw peeled onion at the side of her plate, from which she now and then took a bite, as if she were eating an apple. All of this was very comforting to me.

I loved my grandmother with a passion. I loved my Aunt Mary, too, but she was less forgiving than my grandmother, and I was sometimes afraid of her, especially when she accused me of imagined sexual escapades. It did not help that her somewhat hysterical accusations reminded me of those deliriously happy evenings after my mother's death when my father had taken me to the Royal Hawaiian Hotel for supper.

My grandmother, whose people came from Clare, used language from her Irish past, words that thrilled me with their reminder of my mother. She, too, had heard these strange words and expressions. A balsa wood basket of berries was a "punnet." When my grandmother was angry, she was "vexed." I understood that she was about to speak ill of someone, often with cause, when she began a sentence, "May God forgive me." When in a bad temper, she was "in the briar." She and my aunt both called a woman's private parts "the Black Gethern," and when I asked my grandmother what it meant in Gaelic, she said she didn't know; Black Gethern had always been its name. When I was too brazen for her liking, as when I said that I would never use the term "Black Gethern" as a name for my vagina, she threatened to sell me to the tinkers.

The year before, I had met a young man from Princeton named Singy who was spending Christmas at the Halekulani Hotel in Waikiki with his grandparents, and we had written to each other when he returned to the mainland. He lived on the Main Line, not far from Philadelphia, and as it was summer and he was not in school, he often came to see me at my grandmother's house. He took me to dinner, or to the movies downtown, where we were once shown to our seats by an elderly usher wearing a red uniform and cap whom I recognized was my Uncle Paddy. To Singy's credit, he spoke to my uncle without condescension or embarrassment and I regretted for a moment that I didn't love Singy as much as he cared for me. In September, before he returned to Princeton, he invited me to a Philadelphia tradition called the Bachelor's Ball. My grandmother knew about the ball and was thrilled that I had been asked, seeing it as the opening move in my conquest of Main Line society, forgetting for a moment that I did not have an evening dress or suitable shoes or what my grandmother called an evening wrap or the long white kid gloves she thought necessary for any well-dressed young woman. Although she had not sewn in years, her arthritic fingers no longer deft, she decided that she would make me a dress for the ball. We spent several days going through the fashion magazines that she kept under her bed, marking pages until we at last settled on a floor-length sheath of white crêpe with little cap sleeves, and pockets and neck bordered in silver paillettes. She sent me to the butcher, who gave me a long sheet of brown paper. I was dispatched to Rowell's, where a friend of hers in the millinery department repaid an old favor by giving me a bag of ribbons, feathers, and paillettes. We took the bus downtown to a discount-fabric outlet, where she bought three yards of crêpe, and three yards of heavy white silk faille, with which she intended to make me an evening coat.

My grandmother stretched the butcher paper on the floor and cut patterns of the dress and coat with pinking shears. I separated the hundreds of milky, opalescent paillettes from the entangled strips of ribbon, feeling as if I had been given the first of a series of tasks that, if completed in time, would free me from an enchantment. My grandmother worked quickly, and after two fittings, the dress was finished. I had never seen anything so lovely—the dress of a princess, or a fairy. The evening coat was of her own design, reaching to the floor, with a rolled collar ending in a pussycat bow. White silk high heels were bought, and a pair of gloves were borrowed from the daughter of her old Chestnut Hill employer.

I was both excited and apprehensive, perhaps because of my grandmother's increasingly profligate expectations. I would not know the people there, other than Singy. Despite my childhood dancing lessons, I could not waltz, which worried my grandmother. The dress was ravishing, which may have been why I felt shy in it. Such a disguise had worked for my mother, and my grandmother had no reason to think it would not work again. How was she to know that everything had changed? Girls no longer wore brassieres. I'm not sure that I even knew.

My long brown hair was wound tightly into a chignon at the back of my head. The glistening dress was pressed at the last minute between flannel, the soles of my new shoes gently scored so that I would not slip on the dance floor; the gloves rinsed in soapy water with a drop of glycerin to give them a slight sheen. As I came down the narrow staircase the night

of the ball, I noticed that Singy glanced quickly at my grandmother, who stood next to him at the bottom of the stairs. She
saw his look, but I could tell that she took it for admiration. I
was not so sure.

When I walked into the crowded, noisy ballroom, holding Singy by the arm, I saw that a terrible mistake had been
made. Animated young women, tousled and tanned blondes in
strapless, short, colorful flowered dresses were already dancing. They did not wear gloves or stockings. Many of them had
kicked off their shoes. There certainly were no white faille evening coats.

They noticed me at once—how could they not? Tall, pale,
overdressed, and stunned with embarrassment. Implicit in my
costume was the revelation that I had never been to a ball.
There was some snickering, and a melodramatic double take
or two, and I suddenly understood Singy's troubled expression
when he first saw me, as he wondered if he should warn me
and then decided that it was too complicated, and more important, too late for me to change. I did not look like a fairy
princess, as I'd imagined, but an ambitious country mouse intent on making her way and getting it all wrong. The beautiful
dress, meant to protect me, had instead made me look vulgar.
I followed Singy to a table, where I dropped the coat onto the
back of a gilt chair that immediately fell over with the weight
of it. I hid the gloves under a place mat. Singy and some of his
friends asked me to dance, but the dress was too narrow and I
could barely manage a sedate fox-trot. The orchestra played
"I Want to Hold Your Hand" and "It's My Party," but we did not
dance.

My grandmother waited up for me, as I knew she would,

and when I had changed into my pajamas, I sat on her bed to describe the ball to her, keeping from her my humiliation. I told her that I'd felt as if I were dreaming, which was in some ways the truth. I forgot the gloves at the ball and wrote a letter of apology to the woman who had loaned them to my grandmother, offering to replace them, but she wrote to say that I wasn't to bother, as women no longer wore long kid gloves. I never wore the dress or the coat again, although I kept them for many years.

Michael Kaiser, a childhood friend from Honolulu, was at school at Penn and he would now and then come with a few fellow students to have dinner with us on Sunday, when my grandmother and my great-aunt Gracie Shields would make a traditional Irish dinner of smoked salmon and buttered black bread, corned beef and cabbage, mashed potatoes, and soda bread with caraway seeds. I would be sent shortly before they arrived to the Irish bar at the corner to buy cold bottles of porter. Sometimes we would be so full we had to sit in the small, suddenly crowded living room to recover ourselves for an hour or two before Mike and his friends returned to school. My grandmother associated a person's worth with the quality and condition of his shoes, often to my embarrassment openly scrutinizing the heels and toes of the shoes of my occasional visitor. If she determined that a young man's shoes were not sufficiently clean or well kept—they did not have to be new; she was too snobbish for that—with a shine to them and good heels and soles, she did not hesitate to show her disapproval. The shoes of Mike and his friends, fortunately, did not distress her. She could be unpleasant when she decided that a pair of shoes were not good enough for me.

I spent most weekends at the house of my Aunt Pat, who was my mother's youngest sister. She lived in a new suburb of Philadelphia with her husband and four of the ten children she would one day bear. Her house was full of gaiety, and I had to fight the envy that I sometimes felt of happy children. My aunt told me things that I later wished I did not know. She said that my father had once visited my mother in the hospital, where he spent the afternoon with her, having promised that his love affair with a girl named Christmas had ended and that he would never see her again. He said that he loved my mother, had always loved her, and was ashamed and sorry that he had caused her such suffering. My mother was happy for the first time in a long while, and when he left, she went to the window to watch him walk across the parking lot of the hospital. He was driving her blue convertible that day, and there, sitting in the car, was the girl.

MY GRANDMOTHER HAD taught me to dance an Irish jig when I was a child, and she would ask me of an evening, after my aunt, exhausted after her tumultuous day in the emergency room, had gone upstairs to bed, to dance for her. She sang "Marie's Wedding," keeping time with her slipper while I leapt awkwardly about the room, singing along with her, "Step ye gladly as ye go," hands on my hips, legs flailing wildly. But most of all, she liked me to tell her stories about my mother, especially those that described the last few months of her life. I could not tell my grandmother the truth, which limited my material, but fortunately, she did not mind hearing the same stories over and over again. My mother had been her favorite child.

My family moved to Portlock in 1957, when I was eleven years old. It was a quiet and isolated community an hour east of Honolulu, with modest and some less modest houses on either side of a long road set between Maunalua Bay and the low stone walls of the large pond where Hawaiian chiefs had once kept mullet and other fish. Beyond Portlock were the few ramshackle pig farms of Lunalilo Home Road and a dome-shaped extinct volcano named Koko Head. A derelict rusty tram track ran up the side of Koko Head, and on the hill behind our house there were cement bunkers used as lookouts during the Second World War. The bus from town went no farther than Lunalilo Home Road, and once past the dilapidated bar with a blinking sign that read "Okole Maluna," or "Bottoms Up," there was nothing until you reached the small town of Waimanalo, eleven miles away. A short distance to the east was a long and narrow beach called Sandy, favored by bodysurfers, and notorious for a sudden treacherous drop close to shore. If we heard the siren of an ambulance, we knew that someone had broken his back bodysurfing at Sandy. Farther along the coast, at the bottom of a cliff, was Makapu'u Beach, which seemed to be ours alone. It was not possible to park along the narrow cliff road, but there was a patch of sand fifty yards past the beach where you could leave your car and walk to the beach on a rough path of black lava. It was at Makapu'u that I often felt mysterious moments of rapture, and I would remember a cartoon from the *New Yorker* anthology that I was given to read as a child when I was sick, in which a man looking out a window says to his wife, "Look, dear, I'm raining."

Our house, modern and airy in the style of well-designed houses of the Fifties, was on a slight rise, overlooking the Koʻolau Mountains to the north, with the ocean and pond at our feet. There was a big backyard with a few plumeria trees, full of fragrant yellow flowers, the lawn eventually losing itself in a dense grove of kiawe, where my brothers had built a fort so concealed by brush that it could not be seen from the house. A dirt path at the end of Portlock Road ran along the coast, wandering through wild scrubland, across gulches and through dry streambeds until it reached the Point, which, while dangerous, was good for bodysurfing. Rough cement posts marked the ledges where fishermen had been swept from the rocks, warnings that we chose to disregard.

One hot summer, the land around us was suddenly overrun by steamrollers and rock-crushing machines and heavy tractors, making an incessant clanging and banging, and filling the dry air with diesel fumes. My mother soon learned from the maid, whose uncle operated one of the dump trucks, that the industrialist Henry J. Kaiser was clearing the land and filling the king's fishpond in preparation to building a marina and subdivision called Hawaiʻi Kai. Ourselves and everything that we possessed were soon covered in a chalky red dust as the old stands of kiawe were plowed under, and streets of black macadam replaced the king's thousand-year-old pond.

My grandmother knew that Mr. Kaiser had become a national hero after the bombing of Pearl Harbor, when he used his new shipbuilding materials and techniques to build a ship every few days. When I told her that he had also been the first man to put factory workers on the boards of his companies, she said, "Such a nice gentleman. Surely your mother didn't object to a little dust in her hair." I did not tell her that my mother had been too intent on keeping herself sane to mind much of anything.

Mr. Kaiser dressed in outfits of one color, including his socks and shoes, often in hot pink, which was his favorite color, but sometimes in lime green or mustard yellow. I would see him inspecting his new domain, squeezed into the passenger seat of his pink jeep, or riding in a pink truck, as he was quite heavy and it was difficult for him to get around. He had put aside eight acres of land on the way to the Point, where he was building a compound for his second wife, Ale, whose name was pronounced Ally. She was forty years old, tall and beautiful with a large head of thick auburn hair, and a low melodic voice. During the Second World War, she'd been in charge of the outpatient clinic at the Kaiser shipyards in Oakland, and later she became the assistant to the director of medicine at a foundation established by Mr. Kaiser and his first wife, Bess. She had looked after Bess during a long illness, and married Mr. Kaiser a month after Bess died in 1951. She had a son, Michael, from an earlier marriage, whom Mr. Kaiser adopted.

I'd known Michael since the fourth grade at Punahou. We both lived in Kāhala then. As the beach was not good for swimming, Mr. Kaiser had dredged the reef in front of their house to make a swimming hole. I would take a little dip, then cross the lawn to visit Mike and the Samoan boy, Charlie, whom Ale had adopted after meeting him at a pickup softball game in which Mike was pitching. Mike was a lanky, funny boy, very smart, always asking questions and always telling me things (the difference between a slider and a sinker and, later, the difference between Franco and Mussolini). Inspired by the local boys, who were called blah-las, he wore brightly colored bell-bottomed trousers, custom-made for him by a Japanese tailor downtown, and combed his reddish-brown hair into a little quiff over his forehead. I loved him, and we settled on a deep and steady companionship.

My mother had died by the time that the Kaisers' new house at Portlock was finished. In addition to the main house, there was a guesthouse, the boys' house, a house for the servants, two air-conditioned pavilions for Ale's champion standard poodles, a large boathouse, and an orchid house, among other outbuildings. Ale had hired an interior decorator rather than an architect to design the houses, and they had an excessive, even outlandish look about them. The screened orchid house was ruled by a Chinese Hawaiian man named Charlie Wilson, a champion golfer who had taught himself everything there was to know about orchids. He lived in a room in the main house so crowded with every golf and orchid magazine published in the previous twenty years that it had been necessary to cut a small path through the magazines from the door of his room to his bed.

One year, Ale and Mr. Kaiser, whom we called the Boss, went to Argentina on business as the guests of Juan Perón. Ale had admired one of the Peróns' cars, a pale blue Mercedes convertible, and six months later the car arrived at the dock in Honolulu, a gift from Evita. Ale gave the car to Michael, but as he was not old enough to have a license, he drove the car, both hands on the leather steering wheel, from the top gate of the compound to the lower gate, and then back again, many times a day, sometimes allowing me to ride with him.

Although Michael and his adopted brother were sent to boarding school in the east at the end of eighth grade, and I only saw Michael at holidays and during the summer when he was home from Andover, Ale encouraged me to visit her and to swim in one of the large pools on the estate. There was a swimming pool at my own house, but the children were not allowed to use it. My father would dive naked into the pool when he came home from work, and as we could see the pool through the tall windows of the playroom where we had dinner each night, my brother and I claimed the two seats at the table that faced away from the windows. That he was no longer a nice father made his nakedness particularly disturbing. It was as if each evening a vengeful demon noisily disported in the blue depths of the pool. We listened for the splash of his dive and the rush of water as he deftly hoisted himself onto the deck, before we allowed ourselves to open our napkins and eat our dinner.

It was difficult for me to slip away from home to visit the Kaisers, requiring all of my cunning to elude our stepmother for even an hour. She saw to it that our days were crowded with chores whose requirements changed daily, leaving us liable to mistakes and thus punishment, sometimes physical, with no time for play or even solitude. Our stepmother understood that changing the rules every few days left us confused and vulnerable, and, worse than that, afraid. My stepmother and father soon had a child, whose name was David, whom I took for a walk each day to the Point, his stroller jostling and shuddering on the rough path, which he seemed not to mind. Although I was fond of him, I decided that since he could not talk, it didn't matter if he liked it or not.

When I was able to escape, I would race across the newly razed land to the lower gate of the Kaisers' compound, where I would squeeze past the gateposts and make my way to the kitchen. Although I never spoke about my life at home, Ale knew that my stepmother did not feed us enough. The Chinese cook would give me something to eat, and extra food would be put aside for my brothers and sisters. Despite its careful wrapping, the food sometimes left stains on my clothes where I would conceal it, and I would wash my shirt at night in the bathroom sink. It would still be damp when I dressed in the morning, and it was very refreshing until the heat of the day dried it.

After eating in the Kaisers' kitchen, I would hurriedly make my way to one of the pools, where I would swim alone, the stillness causing me to suspect that I was being watched. I was not being watched, but the strain of protecting my brothers and sisters from my stepmother, requiring me to be both devious and resourceful, left me in a constant state of alarm, and my nerves were a bit shaky.

I sensed that beneath Ale's charm, there was a ruthless efficiency, without warmth or sentiment, and I knew to be careful. I was aware, too, that the good manners taught me by my mother were both a form of consideration and a means of protection that served me well in the exaggerated, even fantastical world that Ale had created for herself and the Boss. Not that

Henry J. Kaiser and Alyce Chester on the occasion
of their marriage, Santa Barbara, 1951

I pretended to be other than myself, as my mother once had
done. I was happy in Ale's house overlooking the sea, indulged
and perhaps even loved. As for me, I adored her.

It was well known in Honolulu that the Hawaiian singer
Alfred Apaka, who died before the Kaisers moved to Portlock,
had been Ale's lover. Mr. Kaiser, too, had been especially fond
of Apaka, and the three of them had gone about town together,
and traveled to the mainland and to Europe. Michael told me
that he'd once gone to see Apaka at his house in Kāhala, and
found him naked in bed with one of the beautiful Tahitian
dancers in his nightclub act. This shocked me, as it seemed not
only wasteful, but greedy to have more than one secret lover.
I didn't see the necessity, and when I told this to Michael, he
laughed at me, causing me to sulk all day.

I wondered whether Mr. Kaiser knew that his wife and Apaka had been lovers, and decided that he must have known, and that there had been an understanding between them. She would look after him and he would allow her a private life, provided that he was not humiliated. Perhaps, too, he did not expect sexual constancy from a wife forty years younger than himself who was in every other way loyal and devoted. It was also hard for me in my innocence to imagine how Mr. Kaiser could have sexual intercourse with anyone. That he weighed two hundred and thirty pounds cannot have helped, or so I imagined.

Sometimes he would sit in one of the mother-of-pearl chairs on the lanai overlooking the ocean and pull me onto his lap. He was an intelligent, fair-minded, and honorable man. Michael loved and respected him, and although I liked him quite a bit, I was also a little afraid of him. Each year around Thanksgiving, two jewelers from New York, Mr. Ortman and Mr. Blickman, would arrive in Honolulu carrying black attaché cases filled with their most important jewels. The Boss would ask Michael to help him, selecting a number of things that would appeal to Ale, and she would then be allowed to choose two of them, one for Christmas and another for her birthday in February. She never worried, I realized, that the Boss might make a wrong choice, as Michael understood her tastes very well—sapphires, emeralds, and diamonds, but no rubies.

BECAUSE WE WERE forbidden by our stepmother to mention our mother's name, and all of her books and photographs, even essential household objects like her monogrammed forks and spoons, had disappeared from the house, the younger children began to forget her. There were very few things, maternal or otherwise, that we could hold on to with any assurance. When I looked at the box of photographs my stepmother had yet to find, I realized that there was no longer anyone to answer my questions. Who was the solemn man holding me in the air? Where is the house with the bamboo shutters? There was no one to tell me. No longer any bedtime stories, no more jokes or games. It was then that I began to tell stories to my brothers and sisters, stories that I later told my grandmother, using the scraps and hints that I remembered or had heard along the way, whispering in the dark to soothe them to sleep.

I reminded them that we had once lived in the mountains, but had moved to the beach at Kāhala, where we could be found at our regular table with the green felt top at the nearby Waiʻalae Country Club, playing a few vicious rounds of cards while we ate our lunch of tuna fish on damp white bread. When we were again on the move, Anne, who was a baby, would be settled uncomfortably in the wicker basket of my blue Schwinn bike. I had determined early on that diapers were an encumbrance, especially when they were dirty, so she wore only a shirt, except when we stopped at the club, when she would be bustled into a diaper. Sometimes we would have to stop during the day to clean her, and she and the basket would be vigorously hosed down with cold water each evening when we returned home, a dousing that at first made her scream, but that she grew to like.

If we were kept at home by bad weather or the occasional illness of one of us, we watched 1930s black-and-white cartoons on television, not out of any aesthetic precocity, but because Honolulu was not yet a rich enough market for Mickey Mouse. Certain expressions first heard in cartoons—"Goodbye, cruel world" and "Order in the courtroom, the monkey wants to speak!"—were commonplace in our conversation. In moments of stress or danger, we would sing loudly, "Here I come to save the day, Mighty Mouse is on the way," which reassured us and gave us courage. One television station showed Laurel and Hardy movies, sometimes all day long, and we would sit in front of the television for ten hours. Our favorites, which we must have seen twenty times, were *Sons of the Desert* and *A Chump at Oxford*. Our father would sometimes watch *Maverick* with us on a Sunday night, joining as we lustily shouted the theme song—"Who is the tall dark stranger there? Riding the trail to who-knows-where."

We pushed our way through the hedge at the bottom of our garden to visit the Worthingtons, a family of Hawaiians who lived on the beach. I visited them every day, sitting with the older Worthington girls in the dark Quonset hut where they lived, while they lounged on their beds in white nylon slips or ironed the dresses they would wear that night, all the while complaining about men. I had never heard such talk. The girls were the step-daughters of Mr. Kopa, who was from Maui and the descendant of a high chief. If I had known better, I would have listened to Mr. Kopa's stories rather than spend the afternoon sprawled across one of the beds in the humid Quonset hut, reading the love comics forbidden me by my father.

One winter, when my father and stepmother went abroad for a month, we were looked after by our babysitter, a Filipino girl named Gertrude. It was impossible to anger or disappoint her, and we loved her. She moved without haste, somnolent and a little lazy, with a female heaviness that offered such comfort that even I, who was thirteen, liked to sit as close to her as possible without climbing into her lap.

My father and his new wife cannot have left the island before Gertrude's boyfriend, Benjie, as slender as Gertrude was plump, appeared at the house, carrying a bowling bag stuffed with his belongings. We were delighted to have his company. He sat at the head of the table each evening, wearing our father's silk foulard dressing gown from Dunhill, smoking one of our father's Cuban cigars throughout our dinner of fruit punch, chicken adobo, and Fritos as he threw back mugs of port. He was a bit girlish, using a heavily scented hair treatment called Three Flowers Pomade on a glossy black duck tail at the back of his head. As he was very short, the dressing gown, growing more and more soiled, flowed around his bare legs and feet when he left the table. He would then arrange himself at our father's desk, where he read a magazine called *Modern Man* before retiring early with Gertrude to our parents' bedroom. Sometimes he grew a little impatient with idleness, and chided me if I forgot to play the Filipino love songs he preferred as dinner music, but I didn't mind. We swam in the pool every afternoon and sometimes at night, careening from the board in a raucous competition of backflips and swan dives. We used the telephone to call our surprised friends. As Gertrude and Benjie preferred to sleep late, we had the leftovers of Gertrude's specialty for breakfast, made the night before with soda crackers, two cans of condensed milk, a jar of Maraschino cherries, and gelatin, waking Benjie at the latest possible minute to drive us at excessive speed to school. We were once again a family.

Our high spirits, however, caused us to be careless. We had yet to discover that our stepsister, watchful and silent, was a spy who would betray us. We did not know that our father kept a journal of his expensive wines, or that he might notice the hot sauce stains on his dressing gown. As it grew closer to the time that our father and stepmother would return, we did our best to clean the house, erasing the more visible signs of our revelry, but, as was inevitable, Gertrude and Benjie were found out, and she was fired. She had once threatened a sui-cide "pack," as she put it, if she were ever separated from us, so a few months later, when I secretly visited them in their little apartment in Chinatown, I was relieved to see that she was not only happy but pregnant. Benjie asked if the next time I visited I could bring him some of the good Cuban cigars he'd smoked at Portlock. There was no irony or humor in his voice and I realized that our time together did not hold any regret for him. He would do it again, he said, especially for the smokes.

During my last year at Punahou, my father and stepmother announced that they would pay for college provided I went to the state university, to which I applied and was accepted. But I did not want to go to the University of Hawai'i. I wanted, completely unrealistically, to go to Berkeley. It was the time of Mario Savio and the Free Speech Movement, which greatly appealed to me, but which Mr. Kaiser repeatedly warned was Communist agitation. Despite his fears, he wrote to the chan-cellor of Berkeley on my behalf, as my grades were not good enough to apply without some assistance. With my mother's death, I had lost all interest in schoolwork, except for my classes in history and English. There was not a great deal of psychological insight in Honolulu in the Fifties, especially in regard to children, and no connection had been made, to my knowledge or benefit, between my mother's death and my performance at school. My grief did not manifest itself in depression, at least not in school, but in wild behavior. I was embarrassed by the clothes that our stepmother made us wear, and to ease my shame and to make fun of the clothes, I organized a celebration, which I named Paris Frock Day, when my friends and fellow students obligingly wore layers of their ugliest and shabbiest clothes to school (I was suspended for two days). I demanded that our beloved geography teacher, Mr. Powlison, show us his buttocks rather than his prized stamp collection (suspended for one day). When our stepmother took away my brother Rick's and my lunch cards so that we could no longer eat in the cafeteria, my friend Cully drove me to the Chinese graveyard in Mānoa where I collected the offerings of tangerines and almond cookies to share with my brother. I hid a pair of black nylon panties in the Bible of a particularly strict teacher so that they fell to the floor when he opened the Bible to read the morning lesson. I was not suspended for this as, in a gesture of kindness and even good humor, qualities that I had wrongly assumed he did not possess, he did not report me.

During the summer of 1962, when my boyfriend Billy Quinn was home from college, I would sneak out of the house late at night, climbing from my bedroom window onto a thin ledge, where I would balance myself as if on a tightrope before jumping ten feet over a hedge of hibiscus. Billy and I would often go to a bar in Kāne'ohe on the windward side of the island called Honey's, which was owned by the entertainer Don Ho's mother. It was a place known only to local people, and performers from the hotels and clubs in Waikiki would come to Honey's late at night after their last show. People often squeezed onto the small stage to sing or play slack key guitar or dance the hula. It was exclusive in its way, and very Hawaiian. One of the waitresses was a young woman named Marlene Sai, who later became a well-known performer herself, but in those days she would sing in the middle of the crowded room, a tray of drinks in her hands. One night, to my surprise, one of the waiters told me that Don Ho wanted to see me. I followed Ho into a storeroom crowded with cases of alcohol. He asked me my age and I said that I was twenty-one. He pulled a large Bible from the drawer of a desk, and asked me to swear on it. Although I was only sixteen, I put my hand on the Bible and swore that I was of age. He didn't believe me, of course, staring coldly at me for a few moments before he left the room. I wondered why he didn't question Billy, who was nineteen. It may have been because Billy's father was governor of the state. That we were both underage and breaking the law did not deter us from going to Honey's, which we did at least twice a week that summer.

I can only think that my loving teachers at Punahou were waiting for me to pull myself together. I had been at the school since I was six years old. In the second grade, I'd asked my teacher, Mrs. Corcoran, to have lunch with me one Saturday at the Banyan Court at the Moana Hotel in Waikiki, and she had agreed, even allowing me to sign the bill, which seemed perfectly correct, at least to me, but must have been arranged with the hotel by my mother.

Dinner with my Punahou history teacher, Robert Hemmeter,
Diamond Head, 1962

My father scoffed at the idea of Berkeley, especially after he learned that Mr. Kaiser had written to the chancellor, and he asked if Mr. Kaiser also intended to pay my tuition. I was too embarrassed to ask Mr. Kaiser for his help, and so I pretended that I did not care about college.

I told these stories to my grandmother at night when I had washed the dishes and my aunt had gone upstairs to bed, and in exchange she would tearfully tell me something I already knew about my mother's childhood, and then read aloud one of the three letters she had received from my mother after she was dead. She considered it a fair trade, but I was so sad after hearing even one of the letters, each of them full of everyday news and gossip—Rick was learning to play the ukulele, I had written a poem—with no hint that she would soon be dead, that I would have to go upstairs to sit on the toilet until I calmed myself.

TWO

$A$s I had promised to do, I wrote to Ale soon after the Bachelor's Ball, to let her know that I was all right. A few weeks later, I received four large trunks of clothes and shoes. As Ale and I were the same size, even our feet, the clothes and shoes looked as if they had been made for me. There were suits and day dresses, made by Mainbocher, Balenciaga, and Norman Norell, designers revered by my grandmother, including a hot-pink ski parka by Dior with a row of three large black velvet bows running down the front. There were shoes in silk and satin, as well as a dozen pairs of the same alligator pumps in different colors. Like my mother before me, I, too, would be dressed by a generous older woman, slipping without hesitation into an elegant disguise. Unlike my mother, I did not have a plan.

Ale's clothes were beautiful, and I knew that I could not help but look well in them. I liked their feeling of weight, and their expensive austerity. I would put on the white piqué cocktail dress that tied in a tailored bow on one shoulder simply to see myself in the mirror as I paraded before my excited grandmother. There was a long-sleeved stiff black taffeta dress by Norell, its waist cinched by a wide obi-like belt, and Pucci trousers in a patterned blue velvet, flared at the bottom, which I explained to my grandmother, proud that I knew the name, were called palazzo pants. When I now wear these same clothes, a little stained in the armpits and with the occasional moth hole, I wonder how I have held on to them for so long, despite having lost or forsaken so many other things, not all of them tangible.

When I wrote to thank Ale and to tell her that I was looking for a job, perhaps in a bookstore, she telephoned to say that Mr. Kaiser had arranged for me to meet Walter Annenberg, who was the publisher and owner of *The Philadelphia Inquirer* and a few years later would be the United States ambassador to Great Britain. I'd once confessed to Ale that I wanted to be a writer, in particular, a journalist, although I had no training and no experience, other than that of features editor of the weekly Punahou newspaper. *The Inquirer* must have seemed an appropriate as well as a convenient place to begin my career. I made an appointment to see Mr. Annenberg.

Dressed in one of Ale's linen suits, tight, hot pink, sleeveless, I called on Mr. Annenberg at his office downtown, where I arrived soaked in perspiration, having taken the subway for the first time. It was soon apparent that Mr. Annenberg had no interest in me. He barely looked at me. I was there because

Mr. Kaiser had asked him to see me. As wasting his time would be a mistake, I took a breath and told him that I wanted to be a reporter, but understood that I might have to begin by sharpening pencils or sorting mail. He showed no surprise at my offer, nor did he condescend to bring me up to date on the requirements for employment in the newsroom of a big city paper. He listened for a while, then pushed up the sleeve of his jacket to look at his watch, and told me I was hired. I was to come to work the following Monday. I was thrilled, as I was not sure that he even knew my name. I wrote to Ale and Mr. Kaiser as soon as I reached my grandmother's house to tell them the news.

When I arrived for my first day as girl reporter, dressed in an airy, full-skirted, lavender organdy shirtwaist by Norell, I discovered that I had been assigned the job of classified-ad taker. Mortified by what I realized had been my astonishing presumption, I quietly took my place in one of two long aisles of seated women, the rows divided by a shallow trough with a black rubber conveyer belt into which the ads, torn from the women's big typewriters, were tossed when completed. I put on the cumbersome headphones handed to me and went to work, my skirt spilling over the sides of my narrow metal chair.

What might I have done? I wondered as I struggled to feed a heavy roll of perforated paper into the carriage of my typewriter. Returned to Mr. Annenberg's office to tell him there had been a mistake? Refused the job and enrolled in a college correspondence class? Worked my way over thirty years to an administrative job in *The Inquirer*'s human resources department? Within minutes, I was taking lost and found notices and personal ads over the telephone, helping callers to find or to sell or to buy baby strollers, golf bags, snakes, used mattresses, cars, and in one instance, a parrot who could only say, "I just want a bite."

There was no air-conditioning in the ad takers' cavernous hall, and it was very hot. The song "Heat Wave" had been a hit that summer, and it seemed so apt that I wondered if it had been written for Philadelphia. The women with whom I worked, most of them older than me, were not welcoming, except for one woman named Faye, whose kind advice as to union protocol and correct assembly line behavior saved me from further irritating the others. I struggled to get to work on time, unused to the occasionally contrary subway. I hurt my-self one evening when the heel of one of Mrs. Kaiser's alligator shoes caught in a grate and I fell on the subway platform. It took me a while to learn the tricks necessary to meet the daily quota of ads required of each of us, but eventually I was able to work quickly, at the same time breaking the rules by offering the sometimes muddled callers the cheapest way to word an advertisement, thus saving them the unnecessary expense of useless letters, and depriving Mr. Annenberg of a fraction of his income, a small complicit gesture that made me happy.

Although I knew that I would not stay at *The Inquirer*, I had no sense of a future, or a purpose, or even a goal. My mother's death had deprived me of the ability to think more than a few weeks ahead at once. I had a faint sense that beneath the self that I had begun to form, there might be a buried, still elusive self, but I had learned to hush her, and she had retreated into silence.

All through September, my grandmother entreated me to remain in Philadelphia—not that my father had arranged for me to return to Honolulu—in the hope that I would attend a small Catholic women's college on the Main Line called Rosemont, especially as Grace Kelly's sister, who fitted my grandmother's notion of the feminine ideal in that she was rich, pretty, Catholic, and Irish, had gone there. By the time that I agreed, having waited to hear from my father, I'd stalled long enough to miss the deadline for applications. I finally called the school to please my grandmother and to my surprise was given an appointment to meet the nun in charge of admissions. Even more to my surprise, I was accepted.

Although I did not want to go to school, I could see that it offered a solution, as I knew that my aunt worried about what to do with me. She paid my tuition, and although I was a day student and the school was not expensive, it cannot have been easy for her. I was often hungry. I did not want to ask her for money for lunch as she assumed that lunch was included in a day student's tuition. My lunch at Rosemont was a package of four Entenmann's Butterscotch Krimpets, which I could buy from a vending machine for thirty-five cents. I was not comfortable at the school, in part because I no longer believed in God, thanks to a few obscene questions once asked me by a priest in the confessional, and I did not have the benefit of the shared intimacy that comes from living in a dorm. As an island girl who had not worn shoes until I was ten years old, I found the strict rules—stockings had to be worn year-round!—intolerable.

I was at Rosemont when I learned that Kennedy had been killed. We were immediately summoned to the chapel for prayers, and the sound of weeping grew in intensity as the sobbing girls and nuns fell into the crowded pews. By chance, I was to spend the weekend of Kennedy's funeral with my father's sister and her husband and children, relatives previously unknown to me, at their house in New Jersey, a visit arranged by my stepmother, who was still capable of rendering her particular form of sadism even at a distance. It was soon obvious that they no more wanted to see me than I wanted to see them. All I wished to do was to watch Kennedy's funeral on television, but my father's sister and her husband had despised Kennedy and could barely conceal their happiness that our Irish Catholic president was dead. I was forbidden to turn on the television. It was my first experience of that particular kind of hatred, and it made me think about the unkindnesses that my mother must have suffered from my father's family. It was a dismal weekend, and when I returned to my grandmother's house Sunday afternoon, I embarrassed her by covering her with kisses.

After two desultory years at Rosemont, I left Philadelphia against the wishes of my grandmother and my aunts, and took the train to New York, where Ale Kaiser had again found me a job.

THREE

**M**y roommate was a girl I had met at Rosemont. She had found work in New York in a small advertising agency that represented the king of Jordan, whom they called His Tiniest Highness. We lived in a small one-room apartment on East Forty-sixth Street near Second Avenue, with two single mattresses on box springs and a telephone. My roommate's mother, who lived on the Upper East Side, gave us towels and sheets, two plates, some knives and forks, and two coffee mugs. The rent, which we would share, was one hundred and seventy dollars a month. We were both a bit astonished to find ourselves in New York.

As the biggest customer of Bergdorf Goodman, an exclusive

and expensive women's store on Fifth Avenue, Ale Kaiser had called Andrew Goodman, who owned the store, and told him to hire me. No interview had been necessary. As instructed, I went to the employees' entrance on Fifty-eighth Street, next to the Paris Theater, stamped my time card in the pleasantly noisy machine, and took the elevator to the boutique on the sixth floor, where I was to work as a salesgirl.

Bergdorf's in those days was far too grand to have open racks of clothes displayed for the benefit of browsing customers. A saleswoman, dressed in black, would coldly greet a first-time visitor to ask what it was precisely that she hoped to find. While the customer explained that she was looking for a dress to wear to a cousin's wedding, or a warm but not too-warm winter coat, the saleswoman quickly determined whether or not she would make a suitable Bergdorf client. If she did not satisfy the saleswoman's rigid standards of style and class, she would be brusquely informed that the store had nothing for her. The regular customers from New York and New Jersey and Connecticut, some of whose mothers and grandmothers had been dressed by Bergdorf's, were not intimidated or tentative, and they were treated with respect, if not obsequity. Some of them could be unpleasant.

Many of the men and women who worked at Bergdorf's were from Cuba. Mr. Goodman's wife, Nena, said to have been a beautiful nightclub dancer who escaped from Havana after the fall of Batista with the help of a male admirer, made it known among Cubans that if they could make it to New York, they would be given a job at the store. The Cubans told me upon first meeting that in their own country they had been married to doctors or the owners of sugar plantations, or were the daughters of once-powerful senators and judges. Perhaps they had been. They watched one another for any lapse in deference, demanding the respect they believed was owed them. It was one of my first lessons in class distinction. It was understood that we were all working at Bergdorf's for only a short time due to varying degrees of ill chance, and that we would soon be leaving to resume our rightful positions in the world, preferably as rich men or the wives and mothers of rich men. The women, who were not friendly to strangers, were polite to me, which flattered me until I realized that it was my expensive clothes that they admired, incorrectly assuming that I was not a person to be snubbed.

Three young women, my own age or a little older, worked with me in the boutique. A very chic, very trim black woman named Mary Douglas was in charge of us. She wore each day a variation of the same well-cut black suit, which she called a tailleur, with a choker of fat pearls the color of old teeth. She had very strict rules about dress: no prints; no ruffles; no uneven hemlines; no peplums; no stirrup pants; pastels occasionally, although not for her; and, in homage to Fred Astaire, always one thing just a little bit off—styles not found in Mrs. Kaiser's clothes, to my relief, although I had trouble with the thing a bit off. I had confided to her from the first that the clothes were not mine, and had answered her many questions, while noticing that she herself was secretive. I did not know her age, or where she lived, or how she had come to work at Bergdorf's, or what she did when she was not at the store. She did, however, show me a Polaroid of her lover, the actor Douglas Fairbanks, Jr., who was then almost sixty, posing like a muscle man in a bulging black thong. I had never seen anything like the photograph, and I was deeply flattered that she trusted me enough to show it to me, and to me alone. I was also very pleased that after just a few months in New York, I was already sufficiently worldly to be amused, even if the means by which I measured my progress were, at least so far, a bit limited.

As it was not very busy in the boutique, our vaguely defined job was to wander through the store, choosing clothes and accessories that might appeal to the women who frequented the beauty salon next to the boutique, clothes which we would then arrange artfully on a large round table, or suspend from the mirrored walls in the hope of making a rare sale. We were what are now called personal shoppers. The women having their hair and nails done, grateful not to have to go through the store themselves, were often very specific in their requests, asking for a one-piece blue flowered bathing suit in a size twelve, suitable for Bermuda, or a blouse with a Peter Pan collar and sleeves that buttoned at the wrist to be worn for an appearance in divorce court. Occasionally a customer needed a wedding or birthday present, and left it to one of us to choose a gift, delighted not to have to make the decision herself.

The other girls in the boutique, who were working at Bergdorf's until the time, assumed to be short, when they found husbands or, less likely, more prestigious and lucrative work, were dazzling to me. Verde Visconti, haughty and unapproachable, was the daughter of the Italian designer Simonetta and the niece of the film director Luchino Visconti. Beautiful Serena Russell was the granddaughter of the Duke of Marlborough. I was envious that Serena lived in a women's hotel on Lexington Avenue called the Barbizon, where, my grandmother told me, Grace Kelly had once lived, as I knew that I could never afford to live in such a place. A perky girl named Suzy was said to be related to Joan Whitney Payson, one of the owners of the New York Mets. I had nothing to recommend me but Mrs. Kaiser's clothes, which led people to think that I, too, was an heiress.

My weekly paycheck was forty-four dollars, which, after I paid my share of the rent, left me with twenty-two dollars a week to buy food and a few necessities like toilet paper and soap. What little money I could put aside was used to buy standing room tickets at the theater, and I twice went alone to see *Marat/Sade*. After these extravagances, there was no money to spare. I could not ask anyone to dinner or invite them to the apartment, causing the girls who worked with me to find me both aloof and cheap. If I were fortunate enough to be taken to dinner, perhaps by Serena and her dashing father, an American newspaper publisher, I would bite into three or four dinner rolls, then nonchalantly drop them into my lap when I thought no one was looking. One evening on my way home, I saw Serena on the street, on her way, I imagined, to her lovely room at the Barbizon. She hesitated for a moment and then asked, "I've been wondering, what do you do with all those rolls?" I did not tell her that the stolen rolls served to feed me for several days.

That year, Bergdorf's sold for the first time what were called junior-sized clothes, intended for young women, inspired by Carnaby Street and a shop called Paraphernalia, and designed by Mary Quant and Biba, among others. Every few days, I would visit the new department, which was called Bigi, to examine the clothes. They were cut too short in the waist to fit me, but a fuchsia polka-dot miniskirt worn somewhat impractically with a large triangular kerchief in a matching pattern had my attention, as did a pair of clunky plastic shoes with thick cork heels, and a fringed patchwork leather jacket, all of which would have caused Mary Douglas and Ale Kaiser to faint had I appeared in them. One of the hairdressers in the beauty salon had been after me to cut my long hair, offering to do it without charge as he needed practice, and one evening after work, I allowed him to give me the haircut made famous by the London hairdresser Vidal Sassoon. My new haircut came to just below my ears, although one side, falling from a side part, was about two inches shorter than the other. As the longer side tended to fall in my face, I tucked it behind one ear so that I could see. Mary Douglas, whose own hair was worn in a stiff chin-length pageboy held in place with a black satin Chanel headband, and whom for once I had not consulted, fearing she would stop me, pretended not to know me when I appeared the following morning.

My one friend other than Mary, a young Cuban named Jorgé, worked in the fur department. He had once sold a mink coat to a girlfriend of one of the producers of the weekly television program *Hullabaloo*. In the show, young men in flowered shirts and bell bottoms with wide belts and girls in very short skirts, towering hair, and white vinyl boots danced on top of Lucite boxes to the week's top ten hits, with guest hosts like Chad & Jeremy, and Paul Anka. It seemed to me like the perfect job. Jorgé promised to introduce me to the producer, and he did, arranging for us to have a drink one evening at a nearby restaurant called Reuben's. I prepared myself for the possibility that I might be asked to demonstrate my skills by practicing wild Frug-like gesticulations in front of a mirror in one of the boutique's dressing rooms, but I was not asked to perform, despite the waxed monkey-fur miniskirt I had borrowed for the night from Bigi, and I did not get the job. Years later, I learned that the choreographer Michael Bennett and the Broadway dancer and actress Donna McKechnie had been two of the dancers on the Lucite boxes, which may be one reason, among others, that I was not hired.

The growing contentment that I felt at work was not unlike the feeling I'd had as a child when studying a cross-section of a room or building, or when I imagined the life that I would enjoy in a three-dimensional Victorian doll's house. I found refuge in the secret Bergdorf's, one that was invisible to customers, and even to many of the people who worked there. I would wander from the gloomy employees' cafeteria with its smell of boiled hot dogs to the large humming room where the silent tailors and seamstresses sat at rows of sewing machines as they worked on alterations, then to the ground floor to chat with the pretty salesgirls assigned to the perfume counter, where their looks were more likely to attract male customers. At the slightest hint of a headache, I'd drop by the nurse's office for some aspirin, then visit Jorgé in the fur salon to try on some furs. Many years later, when Ale gave me a floor-length Russian sable coat that, to my disappointment, made me look like an expensive call girl, I saw from the name tag sewn into the lining that it had been made at Bergdorf's the year that I spent roaming through the store.

It had become necessary in childhood, or at least I had believed it was necessary, to maintain a keen watch at all times, and because of this, I had learned to rely, not always with reason, on my ability to interpret the slightest word or gesture, in part as a means to control chaos, both actual and psychic. I had tried to teach myself the trick of distinguishing what people said and did from what I thought they intended or desired, but it was at Bergdorf's that I began to refine my instincts. It seemed to me that some people, although not all, were two persons in one, the first a visible representation of himself, with his shadow self hovering nearby to explain all that the first person was not able to tell me. The danger in this theory, of course, is that I felt a compulsion to force people to recognize all that they refused to know, and I had to teach myself to allow others the refuge of ignorance.

Those moments in books when behavior, rather than language, reveals hidden truths had marked the beginning of my education in worldly matters, but the men and women at Bergdorf's were real, not that I was particularly quick to make that distinction. Jane Eyre had been just as real to me. I liked that moment in *The Portrait of a Lady* when Isabel Archer realizes that Mme. Merle was once her husband's mistress when she finds her leaning against the mantel in Isabel's drawing room while Osmond lounges in a nearby chair. And the moment in *The Reef* when Owen first suspects that Sophy and Darrow are lovers because they do not speak when they are alone together.

When I was a child, I was awakened one night by the reverberating twang of steel guitars. My mother was in the hospital, recovering from a miscarriage, and my brothers and sisters were asleep in their rooms. I wandered through the dark house to the screened sleeping porch, where I found a young woman named Christmas, who worked at the hospital where my father was on staff, dancing to a recording of the song "Lovely Hula

Hands." She was a contestant in the Miss Hawai'i beauty pageant, she explained as she lifted the arm of the record player, and she was practicing the hula she had chosen to perform in the talent competition. I saw that she was not a very good dancer, and to my surprise, it made me happy. But why was she in our house? By the time that I returned to my room, I thought I knew.

Although I was not unhappy in New York, I was more homesick than I'd been while living with my grandmother. My mother was always with me. I tried different ruses to evade her—reading worked for an hour or two—but my half-hearted attempts made me feel disloyal and even traitorous. After one particularly lonely weekend in the apartment on Forty-sixth Street, I looked up the address of my father's boyhood friend the writer William H. Whyte in the Manhattan phone book, and wrote to invite him to lunch on a stiff blue correspondence card I bought Monday morning at the Scribner bookstore on Fifth Avenue and Forty-eighth Street. I did not really expect to hear from him, as he had not seen my father in years, so I was surprised when he answered my note, suggesting that we meet in the Palm Court at the Plaza Hotel, which was around the corner from Bergdorf's, rather than the cafeteria on Sixth Avenue that I had suggested with the intention of paying for lunch. I had read his book *The Organization Man*, for which he was famous, and knew that he had written other books, and I had the implausible notion that he might help me to find a job at a newspaper or magazine. I also wanted to ask him about my father, who was in Japan as a young army captain when I was born, and whom I met for the first time when I was two years old at the Whyte farm in Chester County.

My first meeting with my father, who had been in Japan for
two years of the Occupation, Chester County, 1947

Mr. Whyte, who was known as Holly, admitted that he had
been surprised to receive my note, then amused, then curious.
I said that I hoped that he was not too disappointed. When he
smiled politely but said nothing, I decided not to mention that
I was hoping for advice about a job. He didn't have much to say
about my father. I saw him two or three more times. Years later,
his wife introduced herself to me at a party. "I'm here because

Holly used to talk about you, but who *are* you?" she asked. Good question, I thought.

Other than the girls who worked with me in the boutique and my roommate, I knew few people my own age. A young woman who worked at the perfume counter arranged for me to go on a blind date with Warner LeRoy, who owned a restaurant called Maxwell's Plum, and was, she explained, the grandson of the founder of Warner Bros. I had dinner with him in his restaurant, wearing the least aggressively chic of Mrs. Kaiser's dresses, while he talked about Jane Fonda, with whom he was in love. He was dressed in a red-and-brown-check suit, and because he was fat, he looked like a Victorian illustration of Humpty Dumpty. When a man arrived with an armful of forsythia branches for the restaurant, Warner discovered that I had never been to the flower district, which he said I must see that very night. I explained that I needed to be at work in the morning and could not stay out late. When I stood to leave, he said that he would drive me home. On the way, however, despite my asking him to drop me on the corner of Lexington and Forty-sixth Street, he continued to Twenty-fifth Street, complaining that we were too early. As we passed a few parked trucks brimming with small trees and buckets of flowers, I jumped out of the car. It was my last blind date.

It was true that my experience of the city was very circumscribed, mainly limited to a route between my apartment and Central Park South. In part to change this and to force myself to go out, I volunteered to do charity work at Memorial Sloan Kettering, a cancer hospital on York Avenue and East Sixty-seventh Street. I told the woman who interviewed me that I was good with children and she assigned me to the children's ward, where each weekend I pushed a cart of books from room to room. I immediately infuriated the ill-tempered head librarian when I refused to collect any money for books that were overdue. As I did not want to lose my job, I began to pay the fines myself, pretending that the distraught parents of the often fatally ill children had given me the handful of coins I spilled onto the librarian's desk. I was allowed to take out-patients or those who had been discharged on weekend excursions. I soon had a friendship with one of the boys, a sensitive and solemn African American child with what looked like large gray cauliflowers attached to each side of his head. As you were not permitted to have the children in your home, and he did not want me to visit him at his family's house on Staten Island, we took the ferry back and forth across the harbor all day Saturday and sometimes Sunday, too. I worried that someone would make fun of him, but despite the undisguised looks of revulsion that he received, none of which he allowed himself to acknowledge, no one ever said a word to us. When he died, I stopped working as a volunteer at the hospital.

As there were no plastic security locks on the clothes and no cameras, it was easy to steal from Bergdorf's, despite the store detective, a sullen-looking woman with a clipboard who stood each evening at the Fifty-eighth Street door as employees left for the day. I never stole anything, but I did borrow dresses for the night. I had grown aware of the effect that Mrs. Kaiser's clothes had on both the saleswomen and the customers at Bergdorf's, as well as my roommate, who found my clothes hilarious, and on the infrequent occasions when I had something to do after work, I waited until Mary Douglas had left before hiding my own clothes under a skirted table in the boutique and putting on a dress better suited to a woman my age, nodding in a friendly way to the house detective as I made my escape. The following day, having resumed my rich girl's disguise, I would return the borrowed dress to its rack. I once spilled tomato soup on one of the dresses. I could have kept it, but I did not think of that. After an anxious attempt to clean it, I could see that it needed professional care, and with some apprehension I took it to the store's dry-cleaning department. The unsmiling man to whom I handed it, explaining that I'd noticed the mysterious stain a few minutes earlier while showing the dress to a customer, knew that I had stolen it for the night. After a long examination of the spot, including sniffing at it, he snatched the dress from me and said, "Don't try that again, missy." I'd like to say that I didn't.

Much later, when I worked as a volunteer at a women's shelter, one of the responsibilities given to me, as no one else wanted to do it, was to open the locked room that contained dozens of pairs of moldy and misshapen shoes, dresses, coats, handbags, and even hats that the women were allowed to borrow if they had a job interview. As I thought it might give the women confidence, if only for a few hours, to see themselves in their borrowed clothes, I carried a mirror from home and hid it behind the coats. I would turn on the overhanging light and the women and I would slowly and with great care go through the racks. The clothes, which had been donated over the years, did not always fit well and I kept a box of safety pins and two-way tape behind the mirror for makeshift alterations. The women were as transformed by their costumes as I was transformed by Mrs. Kaiser's clothes, twirling for me as I once had done for my grandmother. It was often difficult, requiring much coaxing and a little theft on my part, a gift of a pair of shoes or a pocketbook, to persuade them to relinquish the borrowed clothes when they returned from their fruitless and humiliating interviews.

**A WOMAN NAMED** Leslie Morris was Bergdorf's house designer, with her own salon on the second floor with rickety gilt chairs and little sofas called canapés set along walls paneled in peach silk. I sometimes sneaked into the salon, standing at the back as the women customers settled in the uncomfortable chairs, crossing and crossing again their legs with that particular swishing sound made by silk stockings. Some of them were accompanied by men who I assumed were their lovers—they were too well dressed, too attentive, too smoothly attractive to be husbands—who stood alongside as the women marked on a little tablet the numbers of the dresses they wished to order. Women came to Miss Morris to copy clothes they'd seen in Paris or in magazines, but she also had her own line of couture, which I admired, especially as she liked to combine colors and fabrics that were not customarily used together. I had noticed her once or twice in the store and had avoided her glance, as she was said to be short-tempered and, even worse, to prefer women to men. One day, however, she stopped me as I staggered to the elevator, my arms full of Thea Porter caftans for Barbara Johnson, the plump Polish wife of Seward Johnson who had once been employed by Johnson's former wife as a chambermaid and who was beloved by everyone at Bergdorf's for her exorbitant spending. Miss Morris looked at me for a moment, and then told me to come that afternoon to her atelier on the second floor. Mary Douglas, who was my guide in all things, was not at work that day. I did not want to call on Miss Morris, but I worried that if I did not do as she asked, she would somehow make trouble for me. She had the look of someone who did not take well to disobedience, and I did as I was told.

Miss Morris, who wore a trim dove gray suit with a heavy emerald and gold fleur-de-lys brooch, led me into a brightly lit dressing room, accompanied by one of her aged fitters, a Frenchwoman dressed in thick black wool, including her shoes. I noticed that Miss Morris's short hair, dyed a Colette red, had a bald spot at the crown. As she fitted a cigarette into an amber cigarette holder, she told me to take off my clothes. I was not particularly happy for anyone to see me without my clothes, but I was adamant that no one see me in my underwear. Mrs. Kaiser understandably did not include undergarments in the boxes of clothes that she continued to send me, and my badly frayed underpants and brassieres were brown with age and washing. The old girdle that I was wearing to hold up my stockings rather than to conceal any bulges, although clean, was stained with old menstrual blood. I could not possibly remove my clothes. When Miss Morris again ordered me to strip, a wooden match to light her cigarette burning between her fingers, I refused, my arms held stiffly to my sides, lest she attempt to remove my clothes for me. She looked at the fitter in astonishment, then turned to me as she shook out the match. "You stupid, stupid girl," she said. "I was about to change your life."

The next day, Mary Douglas explained that it was likely that Miss Morris was considering me as a potential model in the couture salon. When I told her that I hadn't wanted

Miss Morris or the fitter to see my old stained underwear, she opened her black alligator handbag and without a word handed me forty dollars. I stopped at Bloomingdale's on my way home and spent hours choosing a flesh-colored girdle, two pairs of Hanes stockings in a color named Sea Oat, two pairs of nylon underpants, which Mary said dried faster than cotton when washed in the shower, and a brassiere a size too small in the hope that it would make my breasts disappear.

Although I preferred to use the employees' staircase in my role as department store spy, I took the customers' elevator twenty times a day in the hope of seeing Miss Morris and winning another chance to change my life. I rehearsed our eventual conversation so often with Mary Douglas that she at last begged me to stop talking about it. As well as the boredom my questions induced, she did not approve of modeling as a job for anyone with even a modicum of intelligence, an opinion I for once chose to ignore.

When, after several weeks, I did not see Miss Morris, I picked a day when Mary was not at work to go to the second floor, where I asked to speak to Miss Morris. She appeared not to remember me when I asked if she was still interested in seeing me without my clothes. To my horror, she said, "Why would I want to see you without your clothes?" I hurried back to the sixth floor, taking the stairs two at a time, and spent the rest of the day sitting on a stool in one of the boutique's dressing rooms, my back to the mirror.

One day, I noticed that two men were following me as I wandered through the store. One of the men made his way to me and with a nod in the direction of his companion, a handsome older man who stood nearby, said that he was an assistant to Huntington Hartford. Mr. Hartford had an interest in hand-writing and wondered if I would mind writing a sentence—"I am in possession of the secret formula"—as well as my name on the piece of stiff white paper he held out to me. Mildly flat-tered by this, I hesitated for only a moment over the spelling of possession, and did as I was told. The paper was carried across the room to the handsome man, who I assumed was Mr. Hart-ford, who looked at it for a moment, and then smiled at me.

One evening as I left Bergdorf's, I noticed that I was again being followed, not by the man who had asked me to write on the paper, but a man just like him. He caught up to me and said that Mr. Hartford had found my handwriting to be revelatory of an unusually fascinating personality. Would I have dinner with Mr. Hartford? Would I be willing at least to meet Mr. Hart-ford? Perhaps at Lyford Cay in the Bahamas? "No strings, all expenses," he said. "Mr. H. likes to have girls like you around." I said no, that would not be possible, and we nodded goodbye. For the next few weeks, he was often waiting on Fifty-eighth Street and one evening he stopped me as I turned the corner onto Fifth Avenue. "Doing a little grocery shopping on your way home? You go to the A&P, I bet. He owns that, you know. He owns all of them." I hurried past him, and he did not, to my relief, come after me. After a while, he stopped waiting for me, and I found that for the first few days, I was a little disap-pointed. Years later, I read in a newspaper that Hartford's then wife had tied up his teenage secretary, called her bad names, and shaved her head.

Now and then I saw a boy whom I'd met when I was liv-ing with my grandmother. His name was Bill. He was about to graduate from Villanova, and in the fall he was moving to

Chicago to attend business school at Northwestern. He was as handsome as he was ambitious and clever, with an ingratiating sometimes swaggering assurance. He was quick to see that which might be to his benefit and he later became a property developer in Boston and San Francisco, but in those days he made a little extra money as a Campbell's soup salesman. My grandmother approved of him. His shoes were good and he brought her cases of tomato bisque, her favorite soup, whenever I visited her in Philadelphia. He must have thought that I was an advantageous person to know, living in New York and wearing clothes that he could see were expensive, and he began to drive to Manhattan on the weekends to take me to dinner. Although he had no particular interest in books or any of the other things that I liked, which tended to restrict conversation, he left me to my own fancies, and did not trouble me with questions or even revelations of his own, possible intimacies that I was not yet ready to reveal or to hear. He was amusing and amiable in a day-to-day way which I found was all that I could manage. I did not take too seriously his ambition, given my own inability, or unwillingness to wonder what lay ahead for any of us.

He was the first man I slept with, mainly because it seemed it was time to get it done. The act itself, when it finally happened, was not surprisingly a disappointment. Not too painful, no blood on the sheet, nothing to hang out the window overlooking the filthy alley between two white-brick apartment buildings. It certainly wasn't pleasurable, except for the relief I felt in having dispensed with the burden of virginity. It can't have been too thrilling for him, either. I didn't know anything, not even that it was conducive to enjoyment if the woman also moved a bit. I had been more deeply influenced than I realized by my prurient reading of such books as *Peyton Place* and *Forever Amber* and *Candy*, drawing from them the inaccurate notion that orgasm was tantamount to a seizure of great intensity, an occasion of convulsive writhing and deafening shrieks and moans. That this did not happen to me during intercourse seemed to be proof of my inability to achieve the necessary level of bliss, although I could come close to it in masturbation. My failure to have what I thought was an orgasm worried and embarrassed me, and while I did not know to pretend otherwise, I hoped that my deficiency had gone unnoticed.

I had been brought up by Catholic women who believed that good girls did not have sexual intercourse outside of marriage, and that when they did marry and were intimate with their husbands, it had little to do with pleasure. My grandmother knew nothing of foreplay or oral sex, or so I imagined. Girls who became pregnant before marriage were said to be bad girls, or whores, as we called them in school. At Punahou, a girl would now and then disappear overnight, perhaps sent to Japan for an abortion, as I later discovered, or to California, where her child would be taken from her at birth, often without her consent. Our teachers, who surely knew the truth, would tell us that the missing girl had mono and had gone to the mainland for treatment. Those girls who were thought to have lost their virginity in high school were whispered about, but I secretly admired them for having the independence of mind, as well as the requisite hormones, to decide for themselves about sex. That they had somehow managed to disregard the terrifying consequences that I had been taught were inevitable with sex before marriage, filled me with both envy and respect.

I've thought about this quite a bit, especially as it took me a long time to free myself from my grandmother's often preposterous injunctions. When I was a little girl, my mother could make my grandmother blush by asking her about the twins she had borne, which caused me to wonder if there was more to having twins than I knew, at least in regard to my grandmother. My mother had convinced her mother that the conception of twins required two subsequent and immediate acts of intercourse, and it was this that caused my grandmother to dance about the room, shouting with laughter. Her delight at my mother's teasing had further confused me, as I had believed her when she explained that sexual intercourse was an unavoidable marital obligation, undertaken like other necessary domestic chores. I was also confused about the conception of twins, adding to my treasure chest of misinformation about sex.

As a young girl, I had constructed, and constantly modified and enhanced, three different fantasies, choosing one of them each night in order to fall asleep. The stories, which involved capture, resistance, and a last-minute rescue, took place in contrived historical settings that I gleaned from my reading and obsessively filled with intricate detail: a Puritan maiden in gray homespun and a modest cambric collar captured by a war party of Indians inspired by the TV character Tonto and, later, Chingachgook, and lashed to a pyre of wood which would soon be set alight, only to be saved by the sudden appearance of a frontiersman in buckskin and a necklace of bear claws; a young Frenchwoman with a charming lisp, eighteen years old, in a diaphanous white muslin Empire dress and Leghorn bonnet, captured in the Bay of Biscay by Barbary pirates and held prisoner until the arrival of a dashing English officer in a tricorn hat; and last, a young Englishwoman taken in a raid on a North African caravan despite her disguise as a Levantine merchant and sold by Bedouin tribesmen to a sinister Turkish eunuch who would mercilessly groom her for the old sultan to whom he was enslaved, only to be rescued by a Yankee diplomat who resembled Errol Flynn, later deposed by Guy Madison. All of these fantasies ended abruptly with my rescue, during which I was treated with great tenderness, having inspired the love of the hero by my own extraordinary courage.

In other fantasies, I was the hero. I had failed to save my mother, but I could make up for that by saving others. I was unable to sit on a beach without maintaining a tense lookout for anyone in trouble, someone whom I would save with my quick and fearless response. Traveling in a car, I was on the alert for any accidents and subsequently injured persons whose lives I would save, tending them at the side of the road with calm efficiency, not to say expertise in triage. In the end, as in my nighttime fantasies, it was I who was saved from drowning at Makapuʻu one morning by a Hawaiian boy who at the last moment grabbed my long hair and pulled me from the current that was taking me out to sea.

AFTER LOSING my virginity to Bill, I went somewhat proudly to a doctor recommended by Mary Douglas to ask for a prescription for birth control pills, which had just become available. When he learned that I was not married, he slid the prescription across his desk with such force that it flew into the air and floated to the floor, and I had to bend to find it, my humiliation complete. When Bill suggested that we marry, I said yes, not realizing that my loneliness was so great that I would have married the first man who asked me.

With my future husband, Bill, Connecticut, 1966

When I told Mary Douglas that I was engaged, she said that she'd clearly been mistaken when she thought that I was not like other girls, which was particularly wounding, as of course I, too, thought I was different from other girls. I knew that I needed care, and that I needed quiet, but I was embarrassed to tell her this. I did not question too closely whether either of these remedies would be provided by marriage, but I hoped that leaving New York in the company of someone who purported to love me would give me the chance to find out. In my grandmother's day, I would have gone into the convent. Instead, I found a small amount of comfort in the delusion that I had all the time in the world to make as many mistakes as I desired.

FOUR

A few days after Bill and I were married, we drove to Chicago, where we moved into a tall brick dorm on Lake Shore Drive for graduate students attending Northwestern University. I knew that it would be difficult to find work, especially as I had not graduated from college. I could type, a skill that had been required of both boys and girls at Punahou, and I could wear clothes, but I couldn't do much else. I still thought about becoming a reporter, but I had at last understood that I would first have to earn a degree in journalism. When I wrote to Ale to tell her that I had married and had left Bergdorf's, she did not trouble to hide her disappointment that I'd not done better than a poor graduate student. Although I had no complaints and was grateful for all she had done for me, I sometimes wished that when I'd first left home she had given me a small allowance with which to buy food, rather than twelve pairs of alligator shoes, but I also understood the difference between giving a person money each month and sending her shoes that you no longer wanted. When, twenty years later, her kindness undiminished, she sent me a large crate of furs—a chinchilla muff and hat, a Russian sable coat, a voluminous black mink cape, a fox stole, a sable-lined brown taffeta evening coat made for her by Halston—I had to borrow money from my friend Annabel to pay the COD postage on the box.

A week after I wrote to Ale, I received a call from a marketing executive at the Aluminum Association, who wished to let me know that I was one very lucky young lady. He wanted to be the first to tell me that I'd been chosen that year's Miss Aluminum. I was mystified, suspecting that it was a crank call, until I remembered that Mr. Kaiser had interests in metals, including aluminum. I was to fly to New York to be fitted for my Miss Aluminum costume, after which my first appearance would be at a boat trade show at the Coliseum, where the Aluminum Association was promoting the use of their product in the manufacture of boats, particularly sailboats. I would be paid one hundred dollars a day, which was a fortune to me, plus my airfare and lodging at a hotel near the convention center. Without giving it much thought, as appeared to be my habit, I graciously accepted the title and went to New York.

The Coliseum was packed with men who'd come to see the new boats. The few women present were models like me. My costume was a tight, sleeveless sheath in a glittering silver material so rough with sequins that it chafed the insides of my arms. I wore silver mesh pantyhose, a bit thick, and silver high heels with wide ankle straps, and carried a long somewhat unsteady wand made of taped-together cardboard tubes, meant to be a trident, wrapped in tin foil and pasted with glitter. When I saw a Miss Panama Billfish Tournament in a towering headdress that caused her to look more like a stegosaurus than a marlin, and a girl in a bikini who represented a designer of expensive yachts splayed on a simulated deck while a sheepish male model in a white tuxedo, flushed with the heat, offered her, hour after hour, a liquid meant to be a daiquiri, which perhaps it was, and which she drank in two desperate gulps, I realized it could have been worse. I did not have to stand in one place, grinning and chatting, but could stagger about with my listing trident, handing out brochures advertising the benefits of aluminum masts and hulls.

The boat show lasted for the weekend, after which there was a dinner Sunday night at '21' for an exclusive group of yacht owners, given by one of the executives at Kaiser, which I was expected to attend, wearing my silver dress and carrying my wand. The men on either side of me, both in blue yachting blazers with crests on the breast pockets, were polite but not particularly thrilled to be placed next to a dazed twenty-year-old girl with streaks of glitter on her face. One of the men asked me, not unkindly, "Who are you supposed to be, anyway? Tinker Bell?" Halfway through dinner, to my own surprise, I began to cry, and ran to the toilet, where the attendant stared at me for a moment before she whispered, "Oh, honey, get yourself home." I did not return to the table. Nothing was ever said about my reign as Miss Aluminum, but Mrs. Kaiser stopped finding work for me.

Soon after I returned to Chicago, I visited the office of the A-plus Modeling Agency and persuaded them to represent me, despite my modest display of five black-and-white photographs of myself taken in high school that I'd found at my grandmother's house. The owner of the agency thought that my given name, Susan, was too suburban for a fashion model, and wondered if I could add a few letters to it and drop my surname, which would make it sound more European, as in Suzanne or Susita. One name that she suggested seemed to fit the new self that I was hoping to create, and with the help of one consonant and one vowel, I became Susanna.

Each morning, I spent an hour making up the face that would go with my new name, laboriously attaching two pairs of fake eyelashes, top and bottom, and drawing a heavy white line in the crease of each darkened eyelid. I would then consult the list of photographers prepared for me by the agency, and begin my round of visits in the hope that someone would be willing to take a picture of me, which I could then use to make a portfolio of images. This portfolio was known as a book, and was displayed when one went on go-sees or attempted otherwise to get modeling jobs.

My husband now and then went to class, although he didn't seem to have much to do in the way of schoolwork. To my relief, mainly because I had no money, but also to escape our small studio apartment, I began to find work, appearing in the occasional catalogue, doing fashion shows, and editorial work for *Playboy*, which did not require that I remove my clothes. I was photographed by Victor Skrebneski for newspaper ads for

Marshall Field's and Saks Fifth Avenue. When Oleg Cassini came to town for a trunk show at Elizabeth Arden, he hired me as a runway model, and that led to work with other visiting designers.

Listening to the photographers and some of the models talk in a familiar, even slightly show-off way about Kashmir and Fès and the ruins at Petra, best reached at sunset by camel, I began to think that being in the world really was the splendid undertaking I had allowed myself to imagine when I was a child, and how limited, how shabby even, my life would be if I did not find a way to reach the library at Ephesus, preferably in the spring. It was not things that I wanted, but the experience of places, as distant and as hard to reach as possible. How I would accomplish this, and what I would do once I was there, had not yet been settled. It was clearly necessary to make an adjustment, to think in a new way, but how to do it?

It did not help that although I had more and more bookings, I was always slightly embarrassed as a model. It was not that I thought I was above such work, but that I didn't think I was very good at it. I felt as if I were getting away with something and would soon be caught. Fashion photographers had not yet reached the height of coolness—that was to come in a few years' time—but they had begun to use the c'mon-baby-fuck-the-camera style of shooting, with the intention of turning a session into a seduction, using the excuse that any excitement evident in a model's eyes would be an added inducement to buy whatever she happened to be selling. It was also a way, at least for the photographer, to get laid. This approach worked with some girls, but not with me, although not for reasons of morality. I wish that it had worked, as it would have meant more jobs and perhaps a little fun, but I was made uncomfortable by the obvious manipulation.

The agency often received requests for models for trade shows, but after my experience as Miss Aluminum, I refused that kind of work. One day, however, there was an assignment requiring four models to attend a private dinner party where the girls would dress as French maids. The rich young society couple who were giving the party were well known in Chicago, I was told, and thought to be perfectly respectable, perhaps because they were so rich. As we would be paid well, and because I knew the other models, I accepted the job, arriving at the couple's town house dressed in the costume that had been provided for each of us—black fishnet stockings, black patent-leather high heels, a maid's black uniform, very short, with a white lace apron, and a stiff white lace cap. Our job was to greet the twelve guests, prosperous and attractive men and women like their hosts, with glasses of champagne, and later to help in the paneled dining room, lit only by candles.

The party grew very lively, and potentially lascivious for the increasingly excited guests. My model friends did not seem particularly uneasy, not because they were available for trifling, but because they, unlike me, thought it was humorous, making me worry that I was turning into a prude like my Aunt Mary. No one was rude to me, or approached me in an offensive way, although one woman asked me to accompany her to the bathroom and was angry when I said that no, I didn't need to go to the bathroom just yet.

I'd already figured out that it did not hurt if people desired you, but I had begun to see that charm itself was a bit of a racket. I wanted to be admired at the same time that I wished to maintain a certain prideful distance. I understood that as a woman I was watched, and that it was important that I learn to perform certain parts. I had perfected a superficial bravery in childhood, and had picked up a forced Sixties glibness when I lived in New York, but not much else.

While I had formed a mostly effective habit of not thinking too deeply about my own behavior, I continued to indulge in intense speculation about the lives of everyone else. I often wished that I had someone in whom I could confide. I had no college friends and my childhood companions, some of them beloved, were so far away as to be lost to me. I'd had no time or even a way to make friends my own age when I lived in New York, and I had not known any girls other than my roommate and the girls who worked with me at the boutique, who were understandably preoccupied with their own lives. I knew no one in Chicago other than the men who took my picture and the women who worked at the modeling agency. Other than a photographer's assistant named Patricia, who became a much-loved friend, I was in almost every sense, and despite the presence of my husband, on my own.

I was increasingly ill at ease in my marriage. It seemed as if there, too, I was not playing my part with much conviction. When I was not passive, I was willful, making decisions without thought of intention or consequence, veering between extremes with no consistency, such as cooking an elaborate Thanksgiving dinner for five of my husband's fellow students on a hot plate to demonstrate that I was an attentive and competent wife.

I seemed to advance in haphazard leaps and jumps, with no steadiness and always a bit out of order, always a little ahead of myself. I began to require evasions simply to get though the day. I was still surprisingly naive, especially about sex, going so far as to confess to my astonished husband with great sobs of remorse that I had masturbated one afternoon when he was in class. I felt particularly guilty because I had assumed that if you were married, there was no need to masturbate. He was amused, rather than appalled as I'd expected, and laughed about it, much to my irritation, for days. My only solace, as always, was in reading. I was as much of a bookworm as I'd been in childhood, finishing one book only to pick up another, often reading through the night, spending weeks on a subject until I'd begun to understand it. I was grateful that I was still able to lose myself in books, sometimes so intensely that I forgot to eat.

The cold winter of 1966, I realized to my shame that I'd begun to wish that my husband be drafted, going so far as to imagine him in Vietnam, where he would be killed in a firefight soon after his arrival. I would open the mailbox in the dorm's common room in the wild hope that I would find a letter from his draft board. I was so frightened by my fantasy, not of Bill's violent death, but that I wished him dead, that I went to the student health center at Northwestern and asked if I could see a psychiatrist. I knew that excessive guilt was yet another manifestation of ego, and that as a neurosis, it was both compelling and occasionally even efficacious, but the pattern had been established in me so early and so deeply that it had come to assume its own logic. As I could not afford what I would have called a real psychiatrist, I had to settle for a resident. He was awkward, dour, undoubtedly nervous himself, and when I said that I longed for my new husband to be dead, he was silent. At the end of the session, I asked if he would please say something. He took a breath and said, sounding a bit disappointed, "Well, you're not crazy, if that's what you're worried about." Although I did not keep my second appointment with the young psychiatrist, I did wonder why I had not tried to get help earlier in my life.

The summer that I was ten years old, during a visit to my Aunt Pat in Philadelphia, I'd whispered to her that my mother now and then behaved in a way that frightened me. Sometimes her feet would swell, and she would try to hide them by pulling the waist of her trousers down to her hips, causing the trousers to drag behind her. The swelling and the dizziness that caused her to stagger as if drunk were caused by the medicines that she was given, prescribed after the breakdown she suffered when she discovered my father's infidelity, but I did not know that.

I was alone with my aunt at the kitchen table, and she took my hand. I made her promise that she would not tell my mother that I had confided in her, but of course she had no choice but to go to her. I was heartbroken, especially as my mother stopped speaking to me and for several days would not even look at me. She had sometimes been impatient with me, or frustrated, but she had never refused to speak to me. I had betrayed her by confiding in my aunt and she could not forgive me. On our way home to Honolulu, we stopped in San Francisco for a few days. My father, mother, brother, and I were in the restaurant at the Mark Hopkins hotel when I collapsed and could not stop crying, my head on the table. My mother sat there coldly, still refusing to say a word, and my father, to my surprise, angrily asked her, "Why are you torturing that child?"

In my mother's Chevrolet convertible, Honolulu, 1954

A few days after our return to Hawai'i, my mother at last began to speak to me, but it was some time before things were well between us, and it would be a very long time before I spoke to another person about her. She asked if I would warn her whenever she was behaving in a way that I thought was goofy, which was the word that I had used in my conversation with my aunt. "You could squeeze my hand twice whenever I am not myself," she said. "It will be our secret." There were many times when I was obliged to squeeze her hand, an arrangement that drew me deeper into complicity, without easing my fear, or her own. The best that I could do was to try to get her home, or out of the room, or into her bedroom, where I would put on an Artie Shaw or Benny Goodman record and we would listen to "Georgia on My Mind" and "Any Old Time," sung by Billie Holiday. Her favorite was Artie Shaw's "Dancing in the

Dark," which she said was about life itself. When she asked me to dance, I would jump into her arms and sing along with her. The words of the songs went through my head for days.

She was in love with my father and his betrayal was more than she could bear. Nothing in her experience had prepared her for such a loss of love. She was thirty-three years old, with five children. She was far from her mother and her sisters. There was no one whom she could trust, which is perhaps why she chose to confide in me.

Every Tuesday that summer, she would put on a sleeveless linen dress, a pair of black pearl earrings with a matching bracelet, high-heeled black patent-leather sandals, and quite a bit of Chanel No. 5 to visit her psychiatrist, Dr. Pershing Lo. His name fascinated me, and I would repeat it to myself over and over again as I watched her dress for her appointment.

As she was no longer allowed to drive, she walked to the bus stop to wait in the hot noonday sun for the bus that would take her to downtown Honolulu. There were no sidewalks and the heels of her shoes sank into the grass. If she was late, she would walk in the road, and people working in their yards or driving past would look at her. Now and then, someone in a car would stop to ask if she wanted a ride and she would politely refuse, and explain that she was walking to the bus stop.

Each time, I suggested that I go with her, and each time she insisted that I had better things to do. Like what? I would ask, and she would smile. I would wait for her at the bus stop in the late afternoon to walk home with her. When school started in September, I caught my own afternoon bus, and each Tuesday

I walked the length of it to see if she, too, might be on it, but I never found her. It is heartbreaking to me even now.

It was about this time that I began to have trouble not only imagining myself, but myself as seen by others. I did not know if I really was the discrete and particular individual that my mother encouraged me to believe I might be, or if I was as unbalanced and amorphous as I feared. My sister Tina and I began to devise various alternative names for ourselves to identify the troupe of fluid and mutable characters who now and then possessed us. One of my names was Dusty Roads, which I thought devilishly clever. Tina settled on the name Brenda, although she carried that particular fantasy further than I cared to carry my own, insisting for more than a year that she be recognized as Brenda and refusing to answer if she was called by her given name. One Christmas, at my suggestion, she and I rose early to open all of the presents under the tree, leaving a jumbled mess of opened boxes and piles of ribbons and wrapping paper, the presents scattered about the room, without identifying tags, some of them lost forever in the chaos. My mother, whose memory of her one Christmas orange was still keen, was very upset. I could not explain why I had done such a thing, which made me seem stubborn and mean, but I was as bewildered by my wickedness as was my mother. Another time, I found thirty-five cents on the window sill in the maids' room, a place I often frequented in search of arcane information, preferably female secrets, such as how to cause a miscarriage by sprawling facedown across a washing machine during its final spin cycle, or a new Frederick's of Hollywood catalogue, and I slipped the money into the pocket of my shorts. That evening, I was so distraught that I confessed what I had done to my mother, who in her sympathetic way quietly suggested that I might want to return the money to the window sill, saying mysteriously, "I know how hard it is to resist thirty-five cents."

As I was in the fifth grade and too old to take the special Punahou bus home from school, I used the public bus for the trip to Kāhala, transferring in Moili'ili at a stop known to be dangerous for girls from Punahou, as the public school girls kept watch for us in order to torment us with threats of violence, and the occasional shove. Across the street from the bus stop was a shaved ice stand and a photographer's studio with pictures in its window of Japanese mail-order brides and pretty Japanese girls in their graduation caps and gowns, and one photograph of an older couple looking uncomfortable and a little angry. One afternoon, I went into the shop. The proprietor, a middle-aged Japanese man, stood behind the counter. He watched me warily as I bowed politely and said good day. When he did not answer, I realized that he did not speak English and that I would have to find another way to explain that I wanted him to take my picture. With a series of grimaces and exaggerated hand gestures, I mimicked both a photographer and his subject. His face remained expressionless, and I tried again. After a long silence, he nodded, and instructed me, using the calendar on the wall behind him, to return the following day. The name of the shop was at the top of the calendar, and as it was presumably his name, too, I bowed and said, "Arigatou gozaimasu, Yoshida-san." I was relieved when he bowed, too.

Portrait taken by Mr. Yoshida in his studio,
Honolulu, 1956

Wearing my favorite dress, I went to the shop the next day.
He took numerous pictures of me with an old-fashioned camera, draping his head in a black cloth after demonstrating the
poses he wished me to assume—a closed fist under my chin,
a forefinger extended along my cheek, my head tilted at an
unlikely angle. When I returned at the end of the week to look

at the proofs and to choose the photographs that I wished him to print, he slid a piece of paper across the counter on which he had written the number 40. I was surprised, as I had not considered how I would pay for the photographs. I had only the dollar that I received each week as pocket money. During the long bus ride home, I decided that I had no choice but to ask my mother for the money. As soon as I reached the house, I hurried to her room. She put aside her book and looked at me in surprise. "Forty dollars?" she asked. When I told her that it was to pay for photographs I'd had taken of myself, she pulled me onto her lap. "Perhaps they will tell you who you are," she said quietly. "Always a good thing to know." She gave me the money and I picked up the photographs. I did not show them to her, and she did not ask about them. I did not show them to anyone, but kept them hidden in a drawer, under my clothes, now and then looking at them for clues and signs, but they told me nothing.

THE IDEA OF divorce or even separation in 1966 was still so novel, so disreputable, that it did not seem possible that I could leave my husband simply because I had made a mistake. At the same time, I persisted in the belief that I could fix things. I knew that I had the capacity for happiness, even joy, but I had somehow misplaced it. It didn't matter whose fault it was—the question was, how could I find it again? I knew only that I had to get a firm hold, and that I was not doing very well. I had read Seneca's essay on anger, and I tried to follow his daily practice of forgiving others and, most particularly, himself: "What fault have you resisted? See that you never do that again: I will pardon you this time." But pardon was not yet possible.

That spring, Oleg Cassini asked me to come to New York to model his new collection on the Johnny Carson show, along with the model Marisa Berenson. Oleg insisted that we wear his extremely snug, brightly patterned jersey sheaths, almost identical to those made fashionable by Emilio Pucci, although less expensive, without brassieres, and he announced on air to a delighted Johnny that the dress I was wearing was "a lovely hostess gown with a very low neckline for easy entertaining." Shouting over the laughter of the audience, he added that his nickname for me was "Missionary's Downfall," causing me to wince, and my grandmother, who was watching the show in Philadelphia, later to ask what he possibly could have meant. She also wondered if I was trying to ruin my television debut, as she called it, by making a funny face.

In spite of this, Oleg, who was fifty-five years old, seemed to me the ideal of sophistication. He had what I took to be an aristocratic, high-bridged nose, and a thin gray moustache. I could see that his own clothes were well made, and he wore, to my mind, that most dashing of masculine accessories, an ascot. He spoke with an accent, as he was said to be an Italian count with a Russian archduchess for grandmother. He had once been engaged to Grace Kelly and was Jackie Kennedy's chosen designer, honors sufficiently sanctified to cause my grandmother to fantasize that should I ever find myself a widow, I might marry him. Later, I learned that as the wife of the president, Mrs. Kennedy could not too often be seen in the clothes of European designers, and Oleg had obligingly copied some of the French and Italian clothes that she selected for herself each season.

After the show, Oleg invited Marisa and me to dinner. In the restaurant, he offered to check Mrs. Kaiser's heavy turquoise-blue suede jacket, but I refused to remove it. In my pride, rather than wear the wrong blouse, I'd decided to risk it and wear nothing beneath the jacket. I hadn't imagined that I would be having dinner with Oleg after the show, and I would only be in New York for one night. The restaurant, however, was very hot, and both Oleg and Marisa, perplexed by my stubbornness, asked why I would not give up my jacket, especially as I was flushed and visibly perspiring. When I finally told them the truth, Marisa smiled and said to Oleg in French, "Qu'elle est mignonne!" which I, not hearing her correctly, thought was a reference to meat. One of many misunderstandings that left me mortified and confused.

After dinner, Oleg took us to a private discothèque called Le Club. Men, too jaded to stare at us, nonchalantly asked us to dance after first exchanging a quick glance with Oleg, whom most of them seemed to know, to make certain he didn't mind. Marisa danced, but I was too hot in my jacket, and had drunk too much to trust myself on the tiny dance floor. Oleg put his arm around me and kissed me on the cheek and the side of my head, which seemed a bit forward in a suitably worldly way, but he embraced Marisa, too, which made it seem all right. He said that as legs were very important to him, he was happy that Marisa and I had good legs. He said that his former wife, the actress Gene Tierney, had such bad ankles, she couldn't be photographed below the knee.

Later when I returned to my hotel, I took a bath and went to bed. It was soothing to sleep alone. No husband. No loud graduate students coming home drunk. As I was falling asleep, there was a knock at the door. It was Oleg, and he asked if he could come inside for a moment. I didn't want to sit in a chair in my nightgown and, after opening the door, I hurried across the room to the bed, sitting against the pillows and pulling the covers to my shoulders. To my surprise, he sat on the side of the bed. I don't remember what he said, but within a minute or two, he pulled the blanket from my chest and lay on top of me, his face next to mine, his breath on my cheek. When I'd read *Peyton Place* in secret as a girl, a scene in which the sound of a man unzipping his pants arouses a girl sitting on a dark beach became a cherished masturbatory fantasy, but if there was the sound of Oleg's zipper that night, I did not hear it. Perhaps, in his elegance, he had a button fly.

I tried to move aside, pushing him with my knees and feet, but his hand was around my neck, pressing me against the headboard. I could feel his shoulder pads through the soft tweed of his jacket and there was the sour smell of champagne mixed with the scent of his cologne. His head was between my breasts, the bristles of his moustache scratching my nipples. He lifted his hips, fumbling in his trousers as he pulled out his penis. I had bitten my tongue, and there was a taste of blood in my mouth.

As he began to moan, I found myself crouched in a corner of the ceiling, my bare feet balanced on the molding as I watched from above. When he lifted himself from the bed with a contented yawn, I felt myself begin to fall, my arms outspread like wings.

"Goodnight, cara," he said as he absently tucked his penis, its tip shiny with semen, into his trousers. He reminded me that we had a plane to Chicago early the next morning for a fashion show at Saks. He opened the door, looked up and down the corridor, and slipped outside.

I flew across the room, wings flapping, to lock the door behind him.

I turned out the lights and took off my soiled nightgown, careful to hold it by the hem. I folded my wings to put on Mrs. Kaiser's blue jacket and lay on the floor in the dark, airless room. At one moment, I decided that I would go to the airport to try to find an earlier flight to Chicago. I had my return ticket. I would never have to see him again. I knew that if I went to the police or to the night manager of the hotel it would mean nothing but humiliation. I reminded myself that my husband was not working and that we did not have any money. Besides, it was my fault. Why had I allowed him to kiss me in the club? Why had I been drinking champagne, first at the restaurant and then at the club? Why had I opened the door of my hotel room? Why had I not been able to stop him?

I realized that it was morning when I heard the slap of the complimentary newspaper as it was thrown against the door. I lifted myself from the floor, cold and stiff. I would be on the plane to Chicago. I would find a way not to speak to him, or even to look at him. He would be easy to avoid as he would be busy with the models before the show, pulling and tugging at the clothes, and switching accessories at the last moment. I would make myself invisible.

As I'd hoped, he didn't give me a thought, not out of shame, but complacency. Saks was not far from the apartment building on Lake Shore Drive where Bill and I lived, and when the fashion show was over, I walked home, carrying the suitcase that my aunt had given me when I left Philadelphia.

Bill liked gossip and was naturally curious about my trip. He was especially interested in the beautiful Marisa, who I told him had been sweet to me, but he was disappointed that I had so little to say. He asked the same questions that my grandmother asked when I called her—is Johnny funny in real life? Did I meet Ed McMahon? It was impossible to answer him.

I felt only the deepest abasement. I despised my passivity, my implied acquiescence, my greed, my moral laziness, my ease of compromise. At the same time, I did not want to be the sort of person whose faults and weaknesses fascinated her too much. That would only be one more thing to add to my list of regrets. I did not tell Bill about Oleg. I never told anyone.

In an attempt to understand myself, I began to read Freud. When I came upon his theory that guilt represents the expression of the conflict between Eros and the instinct of destruction or death, I was lost. What did get my attention, however, was his contention that it does not much signify whether one has killed one's father or has abstained from doing so at the last moment. Ideally, one is going to feel very, very bad either way. Guilt and shame, according to Freud, are both fatal and inevitable. That I understood.

A few months after my twenty-first birthday in December, I received a telegram from Oleg, asking if I would fly to Los Angeles at the end of the week to take the part of a Slaygirl in a new Matt Helm movie called *The Ambushers*. The movie, with Dean Martin playing Matt Helm, would be filmed in Acapulco. Oleg was designing the clothes. He had chosen the Slaygirls who would play Matt Helm's bodyguards, but he was one girl short, and hoped that I would come to his rescue and be the tenth girl. I would be paid five hundred dollars a week, which was an enormous amount of money to me. It did not take me long to decide, and I wired him that I would be in California in a few days' time. He would not, I was sure, remember the night in New York when I changed into a bird.

I already knew in my heart of hearts—surely one of the most seductive of expressions—that it was yet another escape.

———— FIVE ————

I arrived in Los Angeles two days later and took a taxi, as instructed, to the Beverly Wilshire Hotel in Beverly Hills. On the drive from the airport, I could see a few skyscrapers in the distance, shrouded in haze. The streets were lined with modest Spanish-style houses, Arts and Crafts bungalows, and two- and three-story apartment buildings with flat roofs, each with small bits of lawn with borders of croton, lantana, and bird-of-paradise. The brightly painted wood and stucco apartment buildings had names reminiscent of the tropics and for a moment I was homesick for Hawai'i. The trunks of the royal palms were a pale pink in the fading light, and the streets were spotted with the lavender petals of jacaranda trees. I was surprised by the absence of people—no one walking, no one sitting on his front steps, no children playing in the street. Except for the sound of cars, it was very silent. Coming from New York, and then Chicago in winter, Los Angeles was seductive in a way that engendered a mild melancholy, and I realized that I might be happy there.

The taxi turned from Wilshire Boulevard into the hotel's narrow driveway, and two Latino bellboys hurried to help me from the cab. I tucked my taxi receipt into an envelope I'd marked especially for such transactions, and which I never found again. A woman in a gray jersey turban who was waiting for her car, and who I later realized was Rosalind Russell, gave me a smile that seemed full of both admiration and pity.

The hotel was not expecting me. The desk clerk said that they would not have a room until the following day, and even then it would depend on a cancellation. No one from the movie company was there to meet me, as I had assumed they would be, and I explained to the busy clerk that I knew no one in Los Angeles and had no place to go. I did not have a telephone number, or even the name of anyone connected with the movie, other than Oleg. I imagined that he was staying at the hotel, but I did not want to call him. When the clerk pointed out that there were motels nearby, already directing his attention to the guest standing in line behind me, I whispered that I had very little money, perhaps only a hundred dollars after paying for the taxi, and no credit cards. He sighed loudly and asked me to wait, pointing to one of the big leather chairs in the lobby.

Sitting in the cavernous room, the last of the light finding its way through the glass doors opening onto Wilshire Boulevard, it occurred to me that it might have been wiser had I been better prepared. Hold tight, I said to myself. I will be a Slaygirl and I will earn the exorbitant sum of five hundred dollars a week. This is just a little hitch along the way. Finally, one of the bellboys, less attentive than at first, took my suitcase, and with a nod from the clerk, led me to the elevators.

I was put for the night in a broom closet on the fourth floor, used by the housekeeping staff to store bleach, wet rags, toilet brushes, and mops. There was a strong smell of ammonia, cigarette smoke, and mold. A rusty folding cot with a thin mattress was in one corner, beneath a row of hooks holding feather dusters and plastic buckets. The boy dropped my bag onto the cot and looked surprised when I gave him the five moist dollar bills I held crumpled in my hand.

As it was too early to go to bed, I thought I should have something to eat, as I had not eaten all day. I'd spotted what seemed to be a coffee shop in a corner of the hotel lobby and I followed the bellhop to the elevator. MFK was a large drugstore with plate glass windows overlooking Wilshire Boulevard, with a magazine rack and a pharmacy, as well as a soda fountain with leather and chrome stools. Banquettes were set against a wall with large mirrors in gold frames. I'd noticed right away that the faces in Los Angeles and even the bodies were different from those in New York or Chicago. The contented, even cheerful customers in MFK looked as if they were extras in a musical comedy. I had my dinner (tuna fish sandwich on white bread and chocolate milkshake), too self-conscious to look closely at anyone lest they look back at me. As I read the enormous laminated menu for the tenth time, I realized that I was eating in an awkward and mannered way, as if I, too, were in a movie, although unlike the other people in the room, I was not very convincing in my part. Eventually, I had to give up my table. After I paid my bill, tipping too much, I was left with eighty dollars.

I'd been told by the desk clerk that I would have to use the public restroom on the mezzanine. As I made my way to the ladies' room to wash my hands and face, I noticed that he was staring at me from his station behind the counter. I smiled at him, grateful to have a place for the night, but he pretended not to see me.

There was no lock on the door of the broom closet. I took off my shoes and lay on the cot in my dress, having considered all through dinner whether or not I should change into a nightgown, or if I should leave on the one bare lightbulb hanging from a wire, or if it would be wise to steal a glass from the coffee shop in case I had to go to the bathroom in the night. As at Bergdorf's, I would be witness to the behind-the-scenes workings of the night shift of the hotel's fourth-floor cleaning staff, and privy to practices that might have surprised those hotel guests who would have no idea, unlike myself, how things really worked in a big hotel. That other guests might not have a compelling interest in the doings of the night shift did not occur to me.

What I had not anticipated was that the hotel cleaners, most of them young Hispanic men, would come into the closet throughout the night to find a fresh mop or to smoke a cigarette, startled to discover a girl stretched awkwardly along the cot, her stockinged feet hanging over the edge. I wondered if the news spread after the first few visits, as the intrusions seemed to increase in number, as the surprise of my visitors seemed to decrease. I could see that it was humorous and even ironic, and that my night in the broom closet would make an amusing story, even a fitting metaphor, and this helped to pass the time. I was neither worried nor afraid.

The next day, I was given a room along with a handful of messages. Mr. Cassini was looking for me. I had realized that my vow never to recognize his presence was a bit impractical, as I would have to see him now and then, but I would not do more than say one or two words to him. That night, a few of my fellow Slaygirls and I were taken to a new private club in Beverly Hills called The Daisy by Oleg and the associate producer of the movie, a man from New York named Douglas Netter. He was about fifty years old, with liver spots on his small hands and the beginning of a bald spot at the back of his head. He had the look of someone about to smile, an expression that I decided was typically Irish. He was not like my grandmother's brothers, who were hard men, which some Irishmen take as a compliment, but he had their rackety charm and, I suspected, their gift of deception.

I don't remember if it was that night or the next, as I had too much to drink both nights, but Mr. Netter spent the night in my room, I presume engaging in sex. What I do remember is that when he left in the morning, I said, "Just leave the money on the table." It makes me wince even now. He laughed and said, "I'm afraid I'll need a raincheck, I don't have any large bills." Although he had a wife and grown children, and I, too, of course, was married, I became, more or less overnight, his girlfriend.

Dean Martin and some of his bodyguard, the Slaygirls, in
*The Ambushers*. Penny Brahms is on the far right;
I am next to her, Hollywood, 1967

*The Ambushers* is the third Matt Helm movie, adapted from
one of a popular series of books written by Donald Hamilton.
In the film, Matt Helm, an American agent played by Dean
Martin, is in search of a stolen spaceship along with its beautiful pilot, Janice Rule, who has been brainwashed by enemy
agents. The actors Senta Berger, Kurt Kasznar, and Albert
Salmi were also in the film. I could understand why some of
the girls, including myself, were content to be Slaygirls, but I
wondered why the main actors would appear in such a silly
movie. I was disapproving on their behalf, even though, to my
surprise, they did not demonstrate a hint of the embarrassment
I was sure they must feel.

Oleg had held what the movie's publicist called a Once-
in-a-Lifetime International Competition to find the ten most

beautiful girls in the world to play Matt Helm's bodyguards. It did not occur to me that the movie studio or Oleg, for that matter, could not possibly have cared if there were nine or ten girls, especially as the Slaygirls collectively had two lines of dialogue. The publicist explained that Oleg had traveled to many countries to show his newest resort collection and along the way had "borrowed ten delicious ladies from continents across the globe." The one American Slaygirl, other than me, was the girlfriend of the director of the film.

The Slaygirls were allowed to choose their own hairstyles, and I inexplicably settled on a style of two long ponytails jutting from either side of my head, a hairdo I'd never worn before and haven't worn since, as it made me resemble a Pekingese. There were no rehearsals. Our responsibility as bodyguards would be to trot alongside Dean as he fought the forces of evil, often around a swimming pool, wearing one of Oleg's bikinis. My fellow Slaygirls were pleasant and obliging, although not particularly friendly, at least not to me, perhaps because I had quickly set myself apart by sleeping with Doug Netter. One of the girls, Penny Brahms, had been chosen by Oleg in London. She was sixteen years old, with thick, pouting lips and white-blond hair. She spoke in a coy whisper, not unlike her idol, Marilyn Monroe, and had the girlish habit of twirling a strand of hair around her forefinger. Kyra Bester, a haughty girl representing France, was already a successful model in Paris. She seemed taken aback, if not infuriated, to discover upon arriving in Hollywood the ridiculousness of her role, and, as far as I could tell, refused to speak except in French and only to Oleg. She was one of the few Slaygirls who appeared to have a life apart, as her boyfriend from Paris visited her halfway through the shooting, subtly altering the atmosphere and causing us to stare at him. It never occurred to Kyra that I might understand French, and I listened to them gossip about her fellow Slaygirls, including me, in the most vicious of terms. Tomiko, a pale delicate girl from Japan, talked to herself in a barely audible voice, which, as she spoke in Japanese, allowed everyone to ignore her. Although she was lovely, I wondered how she came to be chosen, as she did not in any way resemble the cartoonish image of a Slaygirl. There were complaints in the wardrobe department, made in her presence, that she was too flat-chested to wear the tight-fitting clothes designed by Oleg for the movie. Lena Cederham, more suited to the part, appeared the following year in an article in *Playboy* called "The Girls of Scandinavia." Ulla Lindstrom, who was Swedish, was soon on the cover of *Penthouse*. The Slaygirl from Italy, Annabella Incontrera, later starred in a movie called *The Black Belly of the Tarantula*. The Scandinavian Slaygirls and Penny Brahms in particular were distinguished by their florid beauty, but any other qualities we might have possessed went unnoticed and, in truth, were irrelevant, even to ourselves.

After a week of wardrobe fittings, we left for Acapulco, where we were put into cottages at the Hotel Las Brisas, secluded in a large garden of bougainvillea and hibiscus spread across a low hill overlooking the bay. Acapulco was at once familiar to me—the flowers and trees, the air, the heat, the ocean, and the easy way of the people, most of whom were not white. Unlike the other girls who had to share cottages, I had my own bungalow with a small swimming pool, thanks to Doug Netter. As my aunt's suitcase had been stolen during the trip, I found a tailor in town who made me three pairs of sharkskin Capri pants in navy, white, and pink with a little notch at the ankle, three sleeveless white linen blouses, and two batiste nightgowns. In the market, I found underwear and a pair of

Photograph taken by William Claxton at the
Hotel Las Brisas, Acapulco, 1967

huaraches, as well as everything else that I needed. My past was dropping from me piece by piece, husband, clothes, even my toothbrush.

In the evening, after a day's work of jumping in and out of a helicopter in a Lycra catsuit or riding bareback on an empty beach in a diaphanous evening gown that had been doused with water so as to show my nipples, both activities thought to be very sexy, I would have dinner with Doug and the movie's producer, Irving Allen. Allen was a large, taciturn, toad-like man without noticeable charm, and I liked him very much. I quickly realized that Mr. Allen and Doug depended on me to report the day's gossip to them, information that might prove helpful in the constantly amended negotiations they seemed to conduct hourly with the Mexican government, or in coping with any unexpected crises of temperament demonstrated by the actors or crew members. One of the bribes tendered to the Mexican Film Board had been the employment of a polite young man, said to be a student at a film academy, whose responsibility was to ensure that nothing that might be considered indecent occurred either on the set or in the movie itself. I had learned during my occasional chats with him that his father was an important senator in Mexico City. I mentioned this one night at dinner and was surprised to see Mr. Allen and Doug take a quick look at each other. They had been having trouble with the government about permission to shoot at an army base. The next evening, the young man had dinner with us, and for several nights after that, and permission to film wherever Mr. Allen desired was soon granted.

Janice Rule and Dean Martin lived in large villas on the hill behind the hotel. Dean traveled with an entourage of male friends, among them his agent Mort Viner, who I later realized supplied him with girls and pills, as well as negotiated his contracts. Martin was elusive, lazy, jaded. I was surprised that he was exactly as he appeared on television and in movies. He didn't like to work too hard, and refused to do more than two takes, which irritated the director, who at least pretended, unlike Dean, to take the movie seriously. His sweetness was placidly impersonal. He had no real interest in anyone, and his easy charm, mistaken for intimacy, served to keep those who were not close to him at a distance. Once he decided you were all right, that was enough, and he treated you with playful irony. I had sensed from the start that he did not want to sleep with me, which allowed him to trust me.

Doug Netter and I were often invited to join Dean and his friends at Teddy Stauffer's discothèque after dinner. There was a house photographer at the nightclub, and one night he took a photograph of me dancing with Dean, handing me a few minutes later the five-by-seven black-and-white print fitted neatly into a cardboard frame in exchange for the fifty dollars Doug placed in his outstretched hand. I planned to send the photo to my grandmother in Philadelphia, who had a passion for Dean, even though he was not Irish. The next day, however, Mort Viner asked me if he could borrow the photograph, as Dean wanted to have a copy made for himself, which flattered me. I never saw the photograph again and when I complained to Doug, he looked at me in surprise. I was not so naive, however, as to ask Viner to return it.

A scene with Dean Martin in *The Ambushers* in which a piece
of my clothing disappears each time the train goes through
a tunnel, Hollywood, 1967

During those first weeks in Acapulco, I learned that one's
behavior on a movie set, particularly when on location, had
a long-established protocol, understandably determined by
one's importance. I saw that those people on the set who were
essential yet peripheral—extras, wardrobe assistants, animal
wranglers—tended to become ardent friends during the weeks
of shooting, often isolated on a dark sound stage closed to out-
siders. Those with a modicum of experience knew that once
the filming was over it was unlikely, unless they were coincidentally to work together on another film, they would ever see
one another again, and this allowed for a certain promiscuity,
not only sexual, but in regard to friendship, too. The important
people on the set—the main actors, the director, the production designer, the cameraman—were understood to be unapproachable. An extra might start a conversation with a caterer
or a grip, but never with the director or a movie star, if it was

even possible to get close to him. Sometimes an actor would speak to a lesser member of the crew, perhaps because he or she wanted something. I noticed that some of the actors prided themselves on their ability to get on with the crew, and made a point of drinking tequila with the grips after work, or sleeping with them (grips tend to be young tough guys, and often handsome). The long periods of waiting drove people to speak to those whom they would not customarily engage in idle chat, and to sleep with partners whom, in more conventional circumstances, they would not have given a second look. Misbehavior on location was not only mostly ignored, but expected, an implicit, almost contractual perk that included alcohol, drugs, and sex.

Canvas folding chairs with the names of the actors stamped on the back were positioned on the set each day, although they were seldom used by the stars for whom they were designated, who preferred to wait in their trailers or dressing rooms. As no other chairs were provided, they were very tempting to those of us who had to stand around for hours, wondering when and if we would be needed. The following year, I was cast as a Follies girl in a movie about Gertrude Lawrence. My elaborate and heavy costume, with a floor-length feathered cape and enormous headdress, did not allow me to sit, and during the long wait between takes I would be strapped to a narrow wooden board, tilted at a slight angle and held precariously erect by a supporting plank. That is the closest I ever came to my own chair.

The prop man, discreet, efficient, and without judgment like all good fixers, provided anything the main actors might want—the crossword puzzle from the previous week's *Die*

*Presse*, sports bets, boys, a monkey, or a bottle of tranquilizers, things it might have been thought difficult to obtain overnight, but which presented no problem for him. A light-fingered set decorator was also tolerated, provided any thieving occurred after an object had served its purpose, and was not too obvious—although it has been done, it cannot be that easy to steal a tank or a racehorse.

One day, Dean Martin asked if I would take to lunch a girl named Dee, who had arrived that morning from Los Angeles. When I asked Doug about her, he said that she was on the payroll as a production assistant, according to Dean's contract, which was a way to have the movie company, rather than Dean, give her some money. I changed from my working costume of white leather short shorts and halter top, tam-o'-shanter with red pompom, and knee-high white vinyl boots, and hurried to a popular restaurant overlooking the harbor where Mort Viner had made a reservation for us. Dee shyly took my hand in her two hands when Viner introduced us and said, "My father is a minister, you know." Of course, I did not know, but I was fascinated. Dressed in a long-sleeved shirtwaist dress and white shoes with low, thick heels, she insisted that we sit in the shade, as her fair skin was susceptible to sun poisoning. There was little additional conversation, and it was difficult to get through lunch.

Dee was one of my first lessons in the arcane world of girl-friends. I'd expected her to be sexy and funny, but Dee was a thin, etiolated, washed-out blonde with almost no personality. Until that moment, I'd thought that the job of mistress to a married man who also happened to be famous required at least a little bit of charm. Dee must have had something, but as hard as I tried, I could not find it. Years later, at a child's fancy birthday party in Beverly Hills, I was sure that I knew the mother of one of the children, although I couldn't remember where I had met her, or her name. She was the current wife of a rich man, the heir to a merchant California family. She hastily turned away when someone tried to introduce us, and I realized that it was Dee.

Although Doug was married and I was married, it did not occur to me to discuss with him the terms of our affair. I was a pretty girl, malleable up to a point, discreet, high-spirited, and tolerant. I had quite deliberately, although without conscious design, found a protector, someone who would keep me from Oleg, and who would look after me. It was the next step in an expediency that had begun with Ale Kaiser and then Mary Douglas. Without the means, both emotional and financial, to look after myself, I needed others to help me. Perhaps I'd always known this. Known that it would take something more than I alone could sustain to keep it all in motion.

By the time I'd reached Los Angeles and lay awake in the broom closet at the Beverly Wilshire Hotel, I'd known that I could not stay with my husband. I called him once a week and talked about the movie in a vague, matter-of-fact way. I felt no guilt or shame, only a slightly nauseating sense of dread. Not moral dread, but an anxiety, mostly unrecognized, as to how I would escape my marriage. I had no intention of stealing Doug from his wife. That would have seemed dishonorable, although it was all right to sleep with him. I had no idea how Doug saw our future together, and would never have asked him. I understood that he, unlike me, had no desire to end his marriage. I also knew that I was not just another girl, and that he imagined his life with me to be something different from his usual love affairs, and even potentially disruptive to his marriage, should his wife discover that I was living with him. I knew that he liked me very much. When I asked him if he regretted having taken up with me, he said that he regretted very little in his life, although he liked to feel that he could always change his mind. When I smiled, he asked, "How could I ever regret you?"

It was clear to me that I was not going to be a movie star, or even an actor. If I was not at ease as a model, I was particularly bad as an actress. Dean asked the writers to concoct a scene in the compartment of a moving train for the two of us in which a piece of my clothing would mysteriously disappear each time the train entered a tunnel. Although I had no lines, I was appallingly bad. It is the sort of movie in which the performances are not expected to be good, in keeping with the definition of kitsch, so it was of no concern that I was bad, but even Doug must have seen that any thought he may have had of my becoming an actress was ill-founded, despite his fantasy that I would be the next Kay Kendall, the English actress who had been married to Rex Harrison and had died young. Perhaps because he was amused by my quick chatter, he next conceived the idea that I should have my own talk show, a plan that I fortunately did not take seriously for a moment. I knew that girls became movie stars and talk show hosts who were not good actors or smart talkers, and that in some instances, those particular gifts could be handicaps, but I had no wish to be famous, and no wish to play someone other than myself. Just who I might be, however, was still a bit of a mystery.

One late afternoon, after a swim in the bay, I returned

to the cottage to find my husband, Bill, in the bathroom, wiping the perspiration from his forehead. He seemed very pleased as he stared at himself in the mirror, dressed in a tan ice-cream suit and white linen shirt that I'd never seen before, and a pair of white Converse sneakers without socks. My first thought was that he looked very elegant. I was so surprised to see him that all I could think to say was to compliment him on his looks. He told me with a satisfied grin that he had quit graduate school, walking out of a tedious class in copyright, and headed straight to Saks where he bought the suit with my Saks credit card, and then stopped at a travel agency on Michigan Avenue, where he found a cheap one-way ticket to Acapulco. "I'm going to be your manager," he said.

I quietly reminded him that I was little more than an extra, and that I had no thought of being an actress. Then I heard myself say that I no longer wished to be married to him. That I had realized during my time away from him that I could not be his wife. He stared at me with what seemed a bored reasonableness, then took a few steps toward me, I thought to embrace me, and punched me in the face. I ran to the terrace overlooking the garden and shouted for help. I must have been heard—the other bungalows were separated from mine by only a few hibiscus bushes—but no one came to help me. He dragged me from the terrace, and hit me until I lost consciousness.

Sometime later, a minute perhaps, or an hour, I heard a man shout, "Get the broad out of here." I was shaking with cold. There were ice cubes melting on my stomach and breasts and in my hair, and a taste of salt in my mouth. It was difficult to see, and when I put my hand to my face, it, too, was wet. I was bleeding from my nose and eyes. I heard Doug's voice and tried to stand, only to fall into darkness.

Then there was the sound of women whispering in Spanish. I was in bed. I could hear children's voices, too, and chickens. A woman sat next to the bed. She spoke a little English and told me that she was my nurse and that she was there to look after me. Her name was Iris. She said that she had been engaged by the gentleman who brought me to the women's clinic. The other man, the tall one, had been taken by the police, and an officer would be coming to talk to me. She said that the nice gentleman, the old one, had arranged for a doctor to come from Mexico City to look at my face, as one of my cheekbones was broken. It was painful to speak and I nodded to let her know that I understood her. It hurt to move my eyes from side to side and to turn my head.

I only wanted to sleep, perhaps because I dreamed about my mother. She stood at the open window, slipped into bed beside me, gossiped with the women. I tried to dream of my father. I made him very handsome and tall, with blue eyes and tortoise-shell glasses, but as he really was very handsome and tall with blue eyes and tortoiseshell glasses, it was not like dreaming. I dreamed that my brother Michael sat at the end of my bed, wearing steel braces on his legs. When we were children, my brother Rick and I contracted nonparalytic polio from the Salk polio vaccine we had been given at school. Two days after we'd been incorrectly diagnosed with flu, our brother Michael, who was three, was unable to walk. He spent a year in the hospital, where he was loved for his sweetness and high spirits, roaming the ward in his wheelchair, wearing a Davy Crockett raccoon hat. He recovered, but during that year my mother spent a few hours with him every day. One evening when I was reading in bed, I heard a loud clanging sound that seemed to grow louder as it neared the house. I went to the window and saw my mother's car, its front fender dragging on the ground, come up the driveway and stop under the porte cochère. I could not see her in the fading light, but I heard her call my father's name. I then heard their two voices, not fully, only a word or two, and I ran to the front door, hiding behind it to listen to them. My mother had hit a parked car in a Hawaiian neighborhood nearby, but she had not stopped. My father asked if she was sure that she had not hurt anyone, and she said that no one had been in the car. She began to cry. "I am so tired," she said. A few minutes later, I heard them drive away in my father's car. My mother was not arrested, although perhaps there was a fine, and their insurance must have taken care of any damage she had done.

Not long after, I found her lying unconscious on the floor of her bathroom, her hair thick with blood. I ran to telephone my father at the hospital to ask him to send an ambulance. My brothers and sister were in the garden with Ishi, the gardener, where he would keep them busy for hours, and I ran back to the bathroom and locked the door. I sat on the floor and held a towel to the side of her head. Her silk nightgown was twisted around her body, revealing one breast, and I gently slid the loose strap of her gown onto her shoulder, as if fearful of waking her.

After half an hour, I ran back to the kitchen to call my father again. His voice was calm but exasperated when he at last came to the phone, and I realized that he had not believed me when I'd told him that my mother was lying unconscious on her bathroom floor, blood seeping from her head. That he thought she'd had me call him in an attempt to get his attention. I wondered if he knew of the many nights when she would wake me in the hope that I would call him at the little cottage in Waikiki where he kept his girlfriend. I couldn't imagine that my mother, lost in her torment, could have kept herself from telling him. "Please," I said, "help her." When I at last heard the siren of the ambulance, I unlocked the door of the bathroom and waited for them to take her away.

I AWOKE ONE morning to find Iris fixing her makeup in a cracked hand mirror. I had been asleep for three days, she said. Three days! she said again, holding up her fingers. I asked if I could have the mirror when she was finished, and she shook her head. When I asked once more, she put the mirror on the bed and walked away. My swollen face was black with contusions. A line of stitches, clotted with blood, ran across my forehead in a haphazard path and disappeared in my matted hair. My eyes were suffused with blood.

She returned a few minutes later and handed me a glass of cloudy water with a straw in it. When I hesitated to drink it, she lifted me from my pillow and held the straw to my mouth. It was coconut water, which accounted for its color, and it felt cool in my mouth. I saw that my pillowcase was stained with blood, not necessarily my own. She had filled a rusty enamel basin with water to wash my hands and feet, and as she helped me to swing my legs over the side of the bed, we heard a shout of warning.

The policeman had arrived, a bouquet of wilting dark red roses in his hand. He sauntered through the ward, glancing at each of the women as if he were selecting a dancing partner. Perhaps he was. A young man in khaki shorts followed him, carrying a basket of fruit that was, the policeman said, pointing at me, a gift to the movie star from the mayor. The flowers were from Bill.

The women gathered at the side of my bed. The policeman said that Bill was under house arrest at a youth hostel in town. He wanted to know if I wished him to be charged with attempted murder. The thought of Bill in his new suit and white sneakers confined to a hostel for two days gave me a moment's pleasure, but I had no interest in revenge or even punishment. I knew that I had been given a way out of my marriage, and that is all that I wanted. The officer said that Bill would like to visit me. I did not want to see him, and I did not want him to be charged. The policeman seemed relieved, and the women nodded their heads in approval. The next morning, Iris told me the police had put Bill on a plane to Chicago. That night I dreamed that my mother ate all of the fruit in the movie star's basket.

Doug had obtained a bag of painkillers from the prop man, which Iris kept close to her. I was grateful for the drugs, as they helped me to sleep. The chickens roosted at night on the railing of my bed, which I found comforting, and each morning Iris brushed their droppings onto the floor. In order to stay mildly in the present, I asked her to teach me two Spanish words a day, with the condition that she not teach me elementary Spanish or words to use with servants, but words that she liked to say to herself, which made her laugh. "I'm not crazy!" she said. "I don't talk to myself." As I had been talking to myself for days, I wondered if she thought I was crazy. That is how I came to know *abeja blanca, los lentos crepusculos,* and *el embriaguez de amor.* White bee, the slow twilight, the drunkenness of love. Words, she said, that she had read in a book of poems.

The other patients in the clinic were dependent on family and friends to provide them with food, bedsheets, music, and medicine. Thanks to Doug, a cook from the hotel sent something for me to eat each day. As I was only able to eat soft food and soup, a limitation that the cook chose to ignore, I gave most of the food to the women. As our intimacy grew, there were requests for certain items—flour rather than corn tortillas, chocolate for the children, hot chilies instead of the mild ones meant for me, and bottles of tequila. The alcohol burned my mouth and I couldn't drink it, but they could, gathering at my bedside, the children swarming over my legs and onto my chest. One of the women had lost her arm in an accident, and another, who could not stop bleeding, had harmed herself in an attempt to miscarry. The older children liked to play jokes on me, giggling behind their hands as I pretended to search for the sleeping pills they'd hidden under my pillow. The nights, not surprisingly, were more difficult for all of us.

I could no longer be in the movie, given my appearance, but Doug insisted that I continue to be paid a salary. Almost everyone on the movie had assumed that I was one of those compliant girls idly used on location and then dropped, and they were surprised to learn that I was still around. There had been a few lines in the gossip column of a Los Angeles newspaper and in *Variety* that one of the Slaygirls in the Dean Martin film shooting on location in Acapulco had been badly beaten.

After ten days in the clinic, I returned to my bungalow at the Las Brisas. Doug had ordered books for me, arranging them around the bed, where they waited until I could read them. His capacity for love was one of the most alluring things about him, as promiscuous as I suspected him to be. If I had instinctively chosen him immediately upon my arrival in Los Angeles in the unacknowledged hope that he would keep me safe, he did not fail me. He protected me in ways that I could never have imagined.

As he went to the set each day and then to rushes in the evening, I was alone for most of the day. The maids treated me with a discreet sympathy, helping me to bathe and to dress. Iris came each noontime to change my bandages and clean my wounds. I was grateful for the few hours of her company, and insisted that she share the lunch of avocados and black beans with rice and white cheese that I ordered each day from the hotel's kitchen. I asked what I could give her to thank her for her kindness, and she said that she wanted a dress to wear to church. Rather than ask Doug to find a dress in the market, one that she might not like, I gave her two hundred dollars, more, I knew, than she needed for a dress, and told her that she should choose it herself. She found one and brought it to show me, putting it on and moving around the room like a fashion model. "Like you," she said. "How did you know that?" I asked, but she just smiled.

One night, I had my old nightmare again, waking to find an alarmed Doug shaking my arm. I was screaming, he said. In my nightmare, hundreds of silent men, women, and children stand outside our house in Tantalus in the mountains above Honolulu. The house was sided in cedar shingles, and as the crowd of people methodically clawed at the walls, their hands grow bloody and raw as splinters of cedar pierce their fingers and lodge under their nails.

Once after a nap in which I'd had the dream, I rushed into the library where my mother was writing letters, and picked up the telephone to call the police. She listened for a moment as I told the alarmed dispatcher that our house was under attack, then took the receiver from my hand with an amused look, said a few calming words to the dispatcher, and hung up the phone. I was shocked. She thought that I was play-acting, when I was saving her life. It took me several days to forgive her. My fear, even more than my love, was overwhelming me. It was not long after this that I began to have trouble breathing, and I was sent twice to the hospital with pneumonia. I began to see a chatty allergy doctor who each week scratched a mildly painful grid of welts on my skinny arms and back, testing for possible re-actions to wool, eucalyptus, feathers, dust, pollen, mold, bee venom, and dog and cat hair, all the while making the kind of bad pun he thought might appeal to a child. After six months of mostly benign torture, he announced triumphantly that I was allergic to everything except bees.

As my mother became less and less rational, I, too, began to lose the ability to distinguish between what was real and what was imaginary. When my father rented a beach house at Punalu'u, I grew convinced that I could see parts of bodies on the floor of the ocean, and for some time, and to everyone's bafflement, I would not go near the water. Rather than swim with my brothers and sisters, I visited the local library. When I soon exhausted the section designated for children, I tricked the amiable librarian, a Samoan woman intent on converting me to Mormonism, into allowing me to borrow books from the Adults Only shelves by producing a letter I'd extracted from my mother in which she wrote that the books were for her own use. I read the books in a grove of coconut trees out of sight of the sea. The trees had been planted a hundred years earlier by King Kamehameha IV and it was a cool and shaded place. There was the sound of the trade wind in the branches, and the waxy smell of moldering palm fronds. As I read the books that I'd borrowed in my mother's name, books like *Forever Amber* and *Désirée: The Bestselling Story of Napoleon's First Love*, I could hear the voices of my brothers and sisters as they played on the beach. It was weeks before I could swim again, looking about in fear as I forced myself to slip underwater. To my relief, the severed arms and legs had disappeared.

Despite Doug's company each night, I could feel myself sliding into despair. As I was still not able to read, the days were very long. I asked Iris to put a chair in a shaded corner of the garden, and I sat there each afternoon until dusk when the bats began to swoop around my head. As I grew stronger, I began to swim in the little pool, which was decorated by the maids each morning with hibiscus flowers. One morning, I absentmind-edly wandered into the hotel garden, where I unexpectedly met two of my fellow Slaygirls on their way to the set. They coolly nodded hello, unable to disguise what I thought was a smile at the sight of my face, insufficiently hidden behind sunglasses and a scarf. One day, Penny Brahms came to see me. Doug said she had been spending a lot of time with Dean. She came twice, both times with a bottle of warm champagne, and told me that people had been very surprised when Doug prevented the movie company from shipping me to Los Angeles.

One afternoon, I found William Claxton, the movie's still photographer, by my pool. He was a big, handsome man with a jagged face and a large blond head. He was married to the model Peggy Moffitt, both of them notorious for the photograph he had taken of her in Rudi Gernreich's topless bathing suit. Waiting on the set each day for an actor to leave his trailer, or for a scene to be lit, Claxton, restless and solitary, had fallen into the habit of looking for me, and he had taken many photographs of me, some of them as I swam naked in the pool. Unlike Penny, who found it difficult to look at me, he stared at me without embarrassment or, what would have been worse, pity. With his instinctive tact, he did not ask to photograph me, and I was grateful. He gave me his shortwave transistor radio so that I could listen to a station from Vera Cruz that was on the air a few hours each day. He showed me how to find the station and we listened to a new song by Álvaro Carrillo called "La Mentira," which was played every twenty minutes. Over the next few days, I heard it so often and liked it so much that I began to hear it in my sleep. I seemed to be getting better.

WHEN THE MOVIE was finished, Doug went to New York, where he had an office, and a wife and children who lived in Bronxville, and I flew to Chicago to get a divorce.

In the state of Illinois, there is a six-month waiting period for an uncontested divorce. When the judge reminded me of this in court, my lawyer asked him to grant an exception. The lawyer then, to my surprise, asked me to remove my sunglasses and to turn toward the judge. As my eyes were still red with blood, I looked like a sated vampire. The judge glanced at my disfigured and swollen face and granted me an immediate divorce. My friend Patricia went to the apartment on Lake Shore Drive where I'd lived with Bill to pack Mrs. Kaiser's clothes into boxes that she would mail to me, and the following day I left for Los Angeles.

SIX

I missed my grandmother and I missed Mary Douglas and Ale Kaiser. Mr. Kaiser was sick and I visited him in a hospital in Oakland to say goodbye to him. He died a few weeks later in Honolulu. As Ale had hurt her back in a car accident years earlier and it had become increasingly difficult for her to sit for long periods, she rarely visited the mainland. I spoke to my grandmother once a week, shouting my news as she could no longer hear very well. Mary Douglas did not answer my letters.

During one of his visits from New York, Doug suggested that he become my manager. He thought that something could be made of me, regardless of my absence of talent, although he didn't say as much, convinced, I assumed, that it didn't matter.

He also wanted to give me a hundred dollars a week, which his production company would pay me, as well as lease me a car. I agreed and we signed a contract.

We lived in a suite at the Beverly Wilshire for a month until I found a small apartment on the corner of Charleville and El Camino, behind the Beverly Wilshire Hotel and across the street from the William Morris Agency. It was on the ground floor of a two-story stucco building in the Spanish style, with whitewashed exterior walls and a red tile roof. The first thing that the owner of the building told me when he showed me the apartment was that a young actress named Kathryn Grant had lived there while seeing her future husband, Bing Crosby. As I was beginning to discover, a provenance of celebrity, preferably connected to the movie business, was highly desirable, and pertained not only to humans, but to pets, automobiles, houses, books, and furniture. A wardrobe assistant on *The Ambushers* had claimed that her high-waisted tan gabardine trousers had been given to her mother by Katharine Hepburn, who may or may not have been her mother's lover. Doug told me that Robert Wagner possessed an enviable reputation for sexual prowess, as he was said to have been taught everything there was to know about sex by Barbara Stanwyck, who was twenty-five years older than Wagner and assumed to know her stuff. It was naturally more prestigious to have been the lover of a movie star or the head of a studio than the girlfriend of a B-list actor or screenwriter, and to have had liaisons with a few famous men and women rather than only one, and it was not considered ill-mannered to refer to past conquests. At Hunter's Books, I found a young employee who always seemed happy to help me. He told me that when he was the high school boyfriend of one of Dean Martin's daughters, Martin's wife, Jeanne, had seduced him. She'd rented an apartment in Westwood for him and fitted it with a king-sized water bed and special blackout curtains for their afternoon meetings, information that he happily offered when I asked for a book by Colette, which led me to assume that he must have been reading on those afternoons when Mrs. Martin was busy elsewhere.

Doug used certain words in reference to sex and to parts of the body that I recognized he once must have used in his marriage, which made me mildly jealous. I consoled myself with the mistaken idea that a marriage was already in trouble if a husband was sleeping with women not his wife. I changed my mind about this later, but the realization that I was in truth a kept woman had a certain glamorous appeal. Doug told me that his brother was a defrocked priest who had married the girlfriend he'd had since he was a seminarian, which led me to think that the Netter boys liked their time in bed and caused me some concern as to my own performance, which I would not have ranked very high. Clearly, Doug had always had girls, and years later I discovered during a chance conversation that my best friend had slept with him after I left him and before she knew me. It was easier for me in bed if I'd had a martini or two beforehand, but I could not claim any skill or even, some of the time, passion. I still knew nothing about sex. Sex was a means to power, not an exercise of desire or a necessary source of pleasure.

I did like to lie in bed to watch him dress. First the crisp white boxer shorts, ironed by the hotel laundry, a shirt, then trousers, long socks, and shoes, and finally a jacket. I had watched my husband dress, but jeans and a sweatshirt had not done the trick, although it might have been the man. For once, there was no association with my father, or so I imagined, as my father had worn aloha shirts and a white hospital coat. I admired the way that Doug extended first one arm and then the other, the tips of his fingers grasping a cuff as he shrugged into his jacket. The way that he put on his watch, the dial on the inside of his wrist, which reminded me of a nurse taking one's pulse. Later, I understood when a friend told me that as a college student he had gone to a burlesque show in New Orleans, where he watched in awe as Lili St. Cyr lifted herself from a bubble bath to dress herself: black lace garter belt, stockings, high heels, Merry Widow, tight skirt, tight-waisted jacket, even a little veiled cocktail hat, before she turned her back to the audience and walked off stage.

At night, Doug and I would go to restaurants that he liked, Dominick's, or Musso & Frank on Hollywood Boulevard, where we would order the same thing each time—a gin martini with olives, then a beefsteak tomato salad and a rare steak. Creamed spinach at Musso & Frank. At night, we would dance in his room to a small phonograph provided by the hotel to Dusty Springfield's "The Look of Love," and Astrud Gilberto singing "The Shadow of Your Smile." It was improbably romantic, and I was happy.

I was exhilarated by Los Angeles. Its easy ways were seductive, the long bright days full of a beguiling nothingness. No overwhelming sense of all that one had not managed to see or hear, which I had sometimes felt in New York. There were few theaters or concert halls or museums, but, perhaps not coincidentally, there were no girdles and no kid gloves.

No thank-you notes, even. I'd been surprised to see women in Saks and Elizabeth Arden in tennis clothes after the formal elegance of Bergdorf Goodman, and to hear expressions I had never heard in New York, such as "it's a definite maybe" and "cursing through your veins," which could be construed, I decided, as more felicitous and certainly wittier, even if unintended, than any correct usage. It seemed a perfect place to begin a new life.

Beverly Hills itself was still a small village, even in 1967, spreading complacently across five or six parallel streets, the town and its suburbs running north to the foothills that separated Beverly Hills from the San Fernando Valley, and south to Culver City. Santa Monica, Westwood, Brentwood, and the ocean were to the west, downtown Los Angeles to the east, its few tall buildings shrouded in smog. There was a grocery store on Beverly Drive called Jurgensen's, which took orders over the phone and made deliveries. A shop on Cañon Drive sold handmade chocolates, and a tiny gallery owned by an elderly gentleman named Harry Franklin sold tribal art and other antiquities. Mr. Franklin allowed me to buy a silver Spanish Colonial shawl pin, an articulated fish dangling from a royal crest, in twelve monthly payments. Doug bought his California clothes at Carroll and Co., on the corner of Beverly Drive and Little Santa Monica, or at a boutique called Dorso, where the window mannequins were dressed in knit golf sweaters, usually pale yellow in color, the sleeves hanging loosely over the cuffs. There were a few big department stores at the foot of Beverly and Rodeo, near the Beverly Wilshire. At Elizabeth Arden, you could take a steam bath in your own wooden box, your head poking from a small hole at the top, while an attendant in a white uniform stood behind you to pack your boiling face in ice, which reminded me of cartoons I'd studied as a child in *The New Yorker*. The manager was a tiny woman named Mary Carlisle, who had been a movie star in the Thirties. She once complimented me on my name, and when I told her that it was not my real name, her eyebrows lifted in an exaggerated expression of surprise. "No one here is called by her right name, dearie," she said. There was a fashionable women's store on the corner of Wilshire and Bedford Drive called Jax, whose owner, a tall flirt named Jack Hanson, also owned The Daisy, the private discothèque on Rodeo. He and his wife, Sally, sold clothes inspired by photos of Brigitte Bardot in St. Tropez—snug Capri pants and cotton sundresses and gingham bikinis. There were restaurants as well as a hardware store, a shoe repair, a stationery, a housewares store that sold gravy boats and silver picture frames, a linen store, a few jewelers, and two bookstores.

After I moved to my own apartment, Doug rented an apartment in one of the high-rise buildings built on the edge of Beverly Hills, near Doheny Drive and Sunset. As he was in New York, he asked me to work with the renting company's decorator. I knew very little then about design and in the end allowed the decorator to do whatever he wanted. Doug was not pleased when he saw what had been done, and I was embarrassed. It seems that his wife was an accomplished decorator. "Well, she could never live here. That's one thing," he said.

He came to town every few weeks, and when he was not there, I did not go out. My isolation was an unspoken condition of our love affair, and it seemed a fair exchange, especially as I didn't know anyone. Random bits and pieces of my old life now and then floated past, some orderly and some not, but never once did it occur to me that it was in fact my actual life that was then taking place, that it had, in truth, begun long ago and was following its inevitable course, day by day, all of a piece and full of purpose. My longing for my mother, ceaseless and untiring, was so fearful that I sometimes wondered if I could bear it. If I was awakened at night by the slightest sound—a dog barking or a branch brushing across a window—I would sit up and call her name, Anne, causing Doug, whose wife was also named Anne, to jump from bed in alarm, his hands clutching his chest.

A few days after I moved into my apartment on Charleville, I had a call from Penny Brahms, who had come to Los Angeles at Dean's request. She certainly was more my fantasy of a movie star's girlfriend than the anemic Dee. He'd asked her to find a place to live, which she had done, and she wanted to show me her apartment in a new building in Hollywood on the corner of La Brea and Franklin.

The building, which had a long circular driveway and a porte cochère attended by a perspiring doorman in a red guardsman's uniform, seemed an unwise choice, as the entrance was very public, and not liable to induce Dean to call on her. The apartment, which had come furnished, was on the twentieth floor. It was not unlike Doug's apartment, especially in its décor. There were glass walls from floor to ceiling, and as we had tea, the lights of Los Angeles began to glimmer all around us. Except for the large white Naugahyde sofa and armchairs, the rooms were filled with things not originally intended as household furnishings. There was a large gilded birdcage filled with silk orchids. The headboard on her bed was an ironwork gate.

The lamps had once served as torches for Venetian gondolas. The dining table was made from the door of a Spanish church. Although the table was set with six Cadiz shell place mats, each holding three sets of glasses, and silverware and china, it looked as if no one lived there. Certainly not six people. Despite possessing what I sensed was a deeper understanding of sex than I could presume, she was surprisingly innocent. She was very pleased with the apartment, so I was, too.

A week later, she called to ask if she could meet Dean at my apartment, as it was more private, and closer to his house in Holmby Hills. We set a time for the next day. I had very little furniture—a glass coffee table bought on time at Sloane's on Wilshire Boulevard, and a double bed, and there were pillows and sheets. I scurried about, picking up clothes and books, and cleaned the bathroom.

She arrived at eleven the next morning and Dean appeared half an hour later, jumping from a car driven by Mort Viner. I nodded hello as I passed him on the walkway and headed to South Beverly Drive to buy magazines, and some candy at Blum's. I liked their caramels and I particularly liked their pink and black tins, which I thought looked very Parisian. I took my time on the way home, ambling along, eating the candy. The mysterious lavender light of my first evening in Beverly Hills had been replaced by a flat shadowless clarity in which color seemed as if it had only recently, perhaps that very morning, been applied. There were no clouds, and everywhere there was the green of lawns and trees and shrubs, all of them neatly tended. Once I turned from Beverly Drive onto Charleville, I did not see another person, other than those in automobiles.

When I reached the apartment, Dean and Penny were gone. I finished the caramels as I washed the sheets.

I knew that I would need more than the four hundred dollars a month that Doug gave me to pay my rent and to buy food, and I decided to return to the one thing I knew how to do. As my face was no longer bruised and my fractured cheekbone and wounds had healed without scarring, I made an appointment for an interview with the Nina Blanchard Agency. They agreed to represent me, and I began to be booked for fashion shows at Saks and Bullocks Wilshire and the May Company. I was sent to Mexico City to shoot an ad campaign for Kahlua, which would appear in *Vogue*. I was photographed for newspaper and print ads for I. Magnin and Saks, and I ran down the Sunset Strip, hair blowing in the wind thanks to an enormous fan mounted on a flatbed truck, for a Budweiser commercial. I was beginning to be known, at least in Los Angeles, which was a small and provincial market, especially in comparison to New York, with very few models who were considered high fashion, as opposed to girls who did the less prestigious catalogue work.

Early one morning when Doug was in New York, Penny Brahms called to ask for my help. She hadn't seen Dean in weeks and she was worried that he had forgotten her. More important, she'd discovered that the last month's rent had not been paid. She never left the apartment, lest Dean arrive unexpectedly. Besides, she said, she couldn't work as her visa had expired. She'd spent her last money on a plane ticket for her mother, who had come from London to visit for a few days— not longer, she explained, in case Dean wanted to see her. She had bought a little dog from a pet store on La Brea, and I could

hear it barking. She didn't understand what had gone wrong. When I asked what it was that I could do, she said she wanted to go home.

I could give her the money for a plane ticket, but I would not be able to give her anything more, and I did not want to ask Doug for money. I called Mort Viner at MCA and asked to see him in his office. He insisted that he take me to dinner at the Luau instead, where he thought we could more comfortably solve whatever it was that was troubling me. He picked me up at my apartment, and on the way to the restaurant offered me a Percodan, handing me the bottle. I took two, not wanting to seem standoffish, or worse, not cool, and put them in my pocket for some imagined future use, preferably alone. "You're from Hawai'i," he said, touching my arm, "you'll be more re-laxed in a tropical setting," which made me wonder.

I had a quick mai tai at the table he'd reserved alongside the lagoon in the center of the restaurant, and then ordered another before explaining to him that Penny Brahms needed the rent on her apartment to be paid, and some money for expenses, as well as a one-way ticket to London. He was surprised. "No problema," he said. He also seemed relieved, and when he ad-mitted that he had been worried all week that I was in trouble, it was my turn to be surprised. "There are worse things than being a few months behind on the rent," he said. He would see to it right away. And he did. She was gone the following week. I don't know what happened to the little dog. I never saw Dean again. Mort Viner called me now and then for a few months, but I did not see him again, either. A few years later, I read in an English tabloid that Penny was by then the young widow of a property developer who had died mysteriously in a plane crash. His will had been forged by his lawyer, and Penny had been left one shilling, four large nude photographs of herself, and her late husband's extensive collection of Dinky metal cars and trucks. She later married a notorious gentleman adventurer named Dandy Kim Waterfield and successfully contested the will, which by then had grown to twelve million pounds.

To ease a melancholy that I often felt, and a longing for the Islands that seemed to increase the farther west I moved, I went every weekend to the beach at Topanga to bodysurf. One Saturday, as I waited for the next set, a man suddenly surfaced next to me. As we watched the horizon, waiting for the right wave, he asked if I would have dinner with him. He said his name was Robby Wald. I pretended that I had not heard him, and swam to shore. The next weekend at Topanga, he again found me and asked if I would have dinner with him and his mother. I said yes.

SEVEN

Connie Wald lived at 615 N. Beverly Drive in a Pennsylvania Dutch–style house built of New Hope fieldstone. There was a small lawn in front, with a border of camellia trees planted by her father. There was a white picket fence at the edge of the lawn, and at the front door, a cast-iron statue of a black jockey in a red jacket, holding a lantern in his outstretched arm.

I arrived for dinner expecting a family gathering. The other guests were John Gregory Dunne and Joan Didion, Natalie Wood, Suzy Parker and Brad Dillman, Deborah Kerr and Peter Viertel (John Dunne, who was my dinner partner, whispered to me as we sat down that Peter's mother had been one of Greta Garbo's lovers), and the film director Billy Friedkin, who was

Robby's friend. We first gathered in a small room where there were a large stone fireplace, a bookcase, a sofa and chairs, and many family photographs, as well as a large drawing of Connie's father, who I at first thought was Albert Einstein. A hinged jaw with white teeth, perhaps that of a shark, hung over the small bar where bottles of wine and alcohol and an ice bucket and glasses were kept. There were drawings by Jean Cocteau on the wall, and two large Toulouse-Lautrec posters. The sofa and chairs seemed to have been chosen for comfort, and there were good reading lights, luxuries sometimes overlooked in rooms of good taste. Connie took me by the hand when I arrived and presented me to each of her guests as if we could not help but instantly admire one another.

Like Ale Kaiser and Mary Douglas, Connie was glamorous. Tall and slender, with a big head, she was fifty years old, with an assured, even practiced charm and easy manner. She was dressed that night in a bright red-and-black Marimekko floor-length skirt and a red cashmere sweater, with big coral-and-turquoise earrings. A wing of stiff white hair flared from one side of her head. During dinner, she now and then looked down the table to smile at me. Later we watched *The Prime of Miss Jean Brodie* in the paneled screening room that had been built for her late husband, Jerry Wald, when he was head of production at Fox. By the end of the evening, I was hers.

I began to see Robby Wald. He was thirty years old, with a hesitant, somewhat mournful smile. He spoke with a slight lisp. It was not his nature to think too deeply about things, perhaps because it had never been expected of him. He drank

With Robby Wald in Connie's dining room, wearing a Gus Tassell
evening gown given to me by Connie, Beverly Hills, 1969

heavily, and would rush to play tennis when he woke with a
hangover, convinced by his previous girlfriend, a yoga teacher,
that any alcohol lingering in his bloodstream would be secreted
from his body when he perspired. He liked to tell me that I
thought too much, and that it was going to get me into trouble,
although what kind of trouble he did not say. I could tell that
he wanted me to be happy, but as he did not know how to make
me so, he decided that the best thing would be to let me do
whatever I wanted to do. Which wasn't much.

He was an agent at the William Morris Agency. His father,
Jerry Wald, had been admired for his unusual success in producing movies that were considered highbrow by Hollywood
standards, and although no one expected or needed Robby to

match his achievements, he felt the weight of his father's reputation. He had little to show for his work, despite a seemingly
inexhaustible social life. I was often astonished at the ease with
which he would telephone a stranger or approach someone he
recognized to invite him for drinks or even to dinner at his
mother's house. An invitation, also to my surprise, that was
almost always accepted. And one, I reminded myself, that I,
too, had accepted. Not all invitations turned out well, however. He once asked Wilt Chamberlain to dinner at a restaurant
in Santa Monica called Chez Jay—how he had come across
Chamberlain in the first place was a mystery; perhaps at William Morris—during which Chamberlain berated us viciously
throughout dinner and called us honkies.

With the death of Jerry Wald a few years earlier, Connie
had married her late husband's doctor, a respected heart spe-
cialist named Myron Prinzmetal. Robby had behaved badly
to Dr. Prinzmetal, contriving never to speak one word to him
during the entirety of his mother's marriage. By the time that
I met Connie, she had divorced Dr. Prinzmetal and his name
was never mentioned. John Dunne, who was full of useful gossip and eager to part with it, told me that Dr. Prinzmetal was
a drug addict. Later, when Connie took me in her gold Rolls-
Royce to visit Prinzmetal in his apartment on Wilshire Boulevard, where he was watched night and day by nurses, I realized
that he was not an addict, but insane. Perhaps both.

I was too cowardly to tell Doug that I was seeing Robby.
I knew that Doug would be hurt and angry, which made me
irresolute and, worse, devious. I would slip from bed to stand
in the dark living room of his apartment, Los Angeles blazing

around me, sleepless with worry. Sometimes he would hear me and come to see if I was all right, and I would think, Shall I tell him now? Shall I tell him? but I would say that I'd had a bad dream and had gone to the kitchen for a glass of water. Although I knew what I had to do, I pretended not to know how to do it.

I had always understood that nothing could come of our love affair, neither a movie career nor a relationship that was not secret, and I had not wished for or expected either of those things to happen. My inability to imagine a future for myself had kept me from thinking too deeply about our attachment. I had misled him, although not intentionally, when I insisted that our arrangement suited me, and I had misled myself. He had given me, unknowingly or perhaps not, the means to move on, even if it meant that I would have to leave him to do it.

I realized that it would make no difference if I told him that it was not Robby Wald with whom I was in love, but his mother, and I at last confessed to him. He wished never to lay eyes on me again. I had used him, he said, and it was true, but not in the way that he meant. I was too lazy, too lacking in the necessary ambition to profit in any calculated way by my looks, or anything else, for that matter. I had believed, as had he, that I accepted the terms of our affair. My sudden abandonment was a shock to him. He asked me to leave his apartment at once, refusing to let me take the few things that I kept there.

In the morning, a box of my clothes and books was left at my front door. I telephoned him, but he would not take my call. Years later, he came up to me in a restaurant in London where

I was sitting with friends and said quietly, "The love of my life," and turned and walked away.

AS WITH Ale and Mary Douglas, my intimacy with Connie began with clothes. Mary Douglas had insisted on maintaining and even enshrining the dress and manners and hairstyles of an earlier decade, but Connie thought that Mrs. Kaiser's clothes were too old-fashioned for Los Angeles, too heavy and too old for me, which of course was true. She began to give me clothes she thought better suited to my age. Some of them were her own dresses and coats, dresses that she had saved from her days as a model for Claire McCardell, and there were evening gowns made by the young designer Gus Tassell. She took me to Rudi Gernreich's studio so that I could choose two or three dresses for myself. We went to a store on Melrose Avenue where she bought her own African dashikis and Moroccan caftans, and soon I was wearing them, too.

She was born in West Virginia near the end of the First World War, and had moved to New York as a young woman, where she became a model. She had adored her father, who was dead. Her cantankerous and alcoholic mother, known as Mammy, lived in an upstairs wing of the house on Beverly Drive, appearing only for dinner with the family, wearing a dressing gown. There was a charming brother, Barron Polan, who was a theatrical agent and producer in New York. That he was homosexual was not acknowledged. She had no particular affection for Robby, but idolized her second son, Andrew, who was her traveling as well as cooking companion. Although she mistrusted gossip, she told me that the Farrow children, who lived opposite to her on Beverly Drive, used to run screaming across the street to hide in her garden, claiming that their father, the director John Farrow, would beat them before an altar he had built in his study. What more I knew of Connie's own life was gleaned from Budd Schulberg's novel *What Makes Sammy Run?* in which the main character, Sammy Glick, an unscrupulous New York press agent who becomes a famous Hollywood producer, was said to be based in part on Jerry Wald. In the book, the woman Glick hopes to marry spends six weeks in Nevada in order to obtain a divorce, walking ceaselessly back and forth across the Hoover Dam with her dog. When I asked Connie if she was the woman who walked across the Hoover Dam with her dog, she looked at me for a long moment and then said, "Yes, but without the dog." It did not occur to me that it was unlikely that anyone had paced back and forth across the Hoover Dam, least of all with a dog, and I was full of admiration.

Forty years later, when she was dead, I had lunch in New York with her two adolescent granddaughters. They were curious about her and asked me many questions. I realized that they did not know she was Jewish, and I remembered a long-ago Rosh Hashanah dinner given by the parents of Robby's friend Richard Roth. When plates of gefilte fish had been put before us, she'd turned to me and whispered, "Look, Sue, fish mousse!"

Although she was friends with society hostesses like Betsy Bloomingdale (Connie loathed Nancy Reagan), she was not intimate with them. Her friends and dinner guests were more bohemian, more artistic, and thus assumedly less dull than the industrialists and rich businessmen and developers and their wives who made up Beverly Hills society, some of whom would become influential members of Ronald Reagan's cabinet when he was president. Theirs was an exclusive and constricted world, provincial despite its pretensions, and surprisingly vulgar. Alfred Bloomingdale's mistress, who claimed that the very overweight Mr. Bloomingdale liked to sit in a custom-made high chair in baby clothes and a bib while she threw cold pablum at him, sued his wife at his death for part of his estate.

A Danish couple, Theodore and Dagne, hired for the evening, served as butler and maid. The food was deliberately simple, long before it became fashionable to serve meat loaf at dinner parties. Toasted pita bread triangles, and an endive salad on crescent-shaped glass plates, then pasta or grilled chicken or vitello tonnato. Dessert was often a pineapple upside-down cake or ice cream with chocolate sauce made by Connie from the recipes of Mildred Knopf. After dinner, guests sat in the living room, where there was a still life by Jean Charlot over the fireplace. Coffee was brought 'round, and more drinks. Then perhaps a movie in the screening room. Everyone was gone by eleven, after Theodore had moved about the room with a silver tray holding glasses of fresh grapefruit juice, a then fashionable hint that the evening was coming to an end.

Connie's guests liked to refer to themselves as Old Hollywood, people like James Stewart and Ray Milland and Raymond Massey and their wives, but there were also relative newcomers, louche adventurers like Ivan Moffat, or the lovely Lenny Dunne, who had been married to Dominick Dunne, with her black hair cut in a Louise Brooks bob. Christopher Isherwood and Don Bachardy would often be at dinner, and

Audrey Hepburn, who was Connie's best friend, with her husband Mel Ferrer, and then with her second husband, Andrea Dotti. There were others, too, members of not so Old Hollywood, like Earl McGrath and his wife, Camilla, said to be a real Italian countess unlike a woman in Beverly Hills who had legally changed her name from Alice to Contessa, and there were the adult children of famous actors and directors, Brooke Hayward and her half-mad brother, Bill, who sometimes arrived in green hospital scrubs with the implication that he'd come straight from the emergency room, although he was a lawyer, and Maria Cooper, the daughter of Gary Cooper, with her husband, the pianist Byron Janis, who was always in a bad mood, suggesting that he was too fine for the company, which perhaps was true. I noticed that Joan did not like to be introduced as Joan Didion, but as Joan Dunne, which was not difficult for me to do, as I thought of her as Joan Dunne. When I once introduced her as Joan Didion to someone who I was afraid would not know her by her married name, she was surprised, and later said to me, "You seem to have forgotten who I am."

There were never any arguments at Connie's dinner table, never any tantrums, much to the disappointment of Earl McGrath, who cultivated trouble. The younger people were on the make, alert, sometimes overly solicitous of the older guests, even a bit obsequious, kneeling alongside the chairs of the more famous of them, perhaps Jimmy Stewart or Billy Wilder, ostensibly to pay tribute, but really to be able to say they had spent an evening with him.

In deference to Connie's belief in what I called the Gospel of Joy, in which nothing distressing or sad ever occurs, I chose to think that the occasional squeeze under the table was accidental. It would not do to lift the tablecloth to see who had put his or her hand on your thigh, or had somehow managed to insert a foot between your legs. Some of the men, even the older ones, were watched carefully by their wives, alert for any potential misbehavior, and I soon learned that should even the slightest bit of flirting occur, it would not be the husband or boyfriend who would be in trouble. One evening when Robert Mitchum saw his wife headed in our direction, gold mesh evening bag in hand, he hurried across the room before she could brush past me, swiping me in the head with her bag, causing a bruise that lasted for weeks.

Jerry Wald had produced one of my favorite movies, *The Best of Everything*, in which my idol Suzy Parker had appeared. One night, the director of the film, a flirtatious Romanian named Jean Negulesco, asked me to lunch the next day at the Brown Derby. I met him there, wearing an enormous hat, which he politely asked me to remove as he could not see my face. He said that I reminded him of a young Grace Kelly, despite my dark brown hair. He promised that if I put myself in his hands, he would make me a star. When I saw him the following week at Connie's, he said that he was expecting me at lunch the following day. I told him that I was not the girl for him. To my surprise, he patted my cheek and said, "That doesn't matter, darling child, we can still be special friends," which made me smile. I did not meet him for lunch, and the next time that I saw him at Connie's, he pretended not to know me.

I was sometimes seated next to Oscar Levant. He had written one of my mother's favorite songs, "Blame It on My Youth," although it was hard to imagine that he himself had ever been young. He was gray all over, with peeling, deeply creased skin, and apparently no spine. He looked as if he were about to slide from his chair onto the floor and then die. As he shakily opened his napkin with contorted and trembling fingers, he would lean toward me and whisper, "Got anything for me, kid?" his tongue wagging behind his jagged teeth. It took me a while to understand that he was asking for drugs, and when I finally told him that I did not have any, he loudly accused me of lying.

Peter Viertel, the writer and husband of Deborah Kerr, sat next to me in the screening room one night and said, *"Are you built for speed or what!"* I had no idea what he meant, and wondered if it had something to do with sex. If that were so, and even if he meant it as a compliment, I did not want to be built for speed. He then asked if I would read a draft of a new short story he'd written. I could visit him at the Hotel Bel-Air, where he and his wife were staying while she worked in a movie. "We'll sit in the garden and talk," he said. I dutifully read the story and went to the Bel-Air. He was charming and, to my relief, well behaved, except when I pointed out, really as an aside, that he had written "noone," when the correct usage is "no one." I would not have mentioned it had he not asked me twice to tell him if there were any mistakes in the draft. He angrily insisted that I was wrong. He asked the front desk to bring him a dictionary, which took a long time to arrive, as they had to send a bellboy to Hunter's Books in Beverly Hills to buy one, and when he discovered that the correct usage was indeed "no one," he was even angrier. I had said many obliging things about his story, some of them not strictly true, so I was surprised that he should be so humiliated over one word. Two words. It was the first time I'd been asked to read a draft of a writer's work and I'd been flattered, and although he'd previously asked me to read more of his new work, it was not mentioned again. So I was learning things; not necessarily about grammar and spelling.

One afternoon, Connie told me that she wished to put me next to Jimmy Stewart at dinner, but only if I promised not to talk about Vietnam. As the war was not a subject often discussed at Connie's parties, I was surprised, but I promised to do as she asked. Early on, I had learned that I was never to speak too earnestly or passionately about politics. When she overheard me ask Shirley Temple if she agreed with Governor Reagan's plan to put welfare bums to work, clearly a question meant to provoke, I was banished for a week to the breakfast room, where nameless houseguests and younger relatives home from college were seated at what was called the children's table.

I did not at first recognize Mr. Stewart, as he was not wearing his hairpiece. He waited until I sat down before taking his own seat, when I heard Connie call out, "Sue, tell Mr. Stewart about your love of dogs!" I turned to him in dread and introduced myself. As we shook hands, he said, "I have a stepson who was killed in Vietnam. He was about your age. Ron McLean. First Lieutenant Ron McLean. My wife Gloria's son. He'd just opened some spaghetti and meatballs when he was shot in the chest. Waiting to be evacuated from a firefight. It was his first patrol." Mr. Stewart talked about his stepson and the war all through dinner. I saw Connie peer down the table at us, pleased by the intensity of his expression. There was little that I could say, and I sensed his relief that I did not condescend to console him. It was not so much politeness on my part, although there was that, but the understanding that anything I might say about the death of his stepson would be platitudinous. He did not need my sympathy, although he knew that he had it. He said that he was a supporter of the war, and that the code name of his stepson's recon patrol, American Beauty, seemed particularly fitting to him. He only stopped talking when we rose from the table and he wandered sadly across the room to his wife. Later, Connie said that she'd known he'd be delighted to talk about dogs, although she hadn't imagined that he'd be quite *that* interested. "He didn't speak to the person on his other side all through dinner," she said, implying that I had caused him to be derelict in his manners. "Dogs will do it every time," she said. I did not disagree, in part because I had no wish to prove her wrong, and because I loved her.

Other nights, I was put next to the elderly Jules Stein, who was an ophthalmologist as well as the founder of the powerful talent agency MCA, which later would become Universal Studios. He would bend stiffly toward me, smelling of Bengay, to whisper that if I could spell the word "ophthalmology," he would give me a present. I could never decide whether he recognized me and didn't care that he asked me the same question each time, or if he had no memory of our last dinner together. Probably the latter. I spelled it correctly, but never received any present, which was a relief. His wife, Doris, who had been a milliner in New York and whose first marriage had been to an army general, details which interested me, was small and plump with a big head of tightly coiffed white hair. I once asked her if I could try on her diamond ring, and after a moment's hesitation, she pulled it from her finger and dropped it into my palm. I put it on and stretched out my hand to admire it. "You will never have jewels, my dear," she said with an oddly triumphant laugh, as if there were a limited number of jewels in the world and my deficiency would mean more diamonds for her. "Never. It's quite obvious. Too bad for you." As it turned out, she was right.

One night when we were having coffee in the paneled screening room, Doris leaned into me on the sofa where we were sitting and whispered that Jules demanded that she lick his ass each morning, and she was sick of it. I looked at Jules, who was sitting across the room, his eyes on a large oil painting of Jerry Wald as he pretended to listen to Connie's son Andrew, and I wondered if she was telling the truth. Not exaggerated metaphors, but the truth. I was a little ashamed that I wanted to know more, but she did not elaborate and I, for once, knew better than to ask. She said that when she recently refused to do it, he tried to kill her by smothering her with a pillow while she was taking a bath. Fortunately, her maid heard the sound of splashing and came into the bathroom just in time. She was often drunk at the end of a party, full of the confidences that alcohol induces, and I doubted if she would remember what she had told me in the morning. When next I saw her, I knew that she did not remember, and I was relieved.

I often found myself alone with Audrey Hepburn, who stayed with Connie when she was in Los Angeles. One evening when I arrived early for dinner, I found her intently examining each piece of chocolate in an enormous box she'd brought

Audrey Hepburn and Connie Wald in the late Fifties

by hand from Switzerland. She selected two chocolates for me, and I ate them. We had been chatting idly for a few moments—I was shy and in awe; she was distracted and probably bored—when she suddenly said, "There is something that I have been meaning to tell you. It will make all the difference in your life, I promise you." Just as she said this, the Filipino cook, Fortunato, ran excitedly into the room with the telephone, tripping on the long cord as he announced loudly that there was a call for her. I left the room so that she could speak in private. Over the next few days, whenever I came across her in the house, I looked at her expectantly, hoping that she would tell me the very important thing that would make all the difference in my life, but we were either interrupted or she was busily on her way somewhere, and I gave up trying. Although she had no edge to her, perhaps the result of a discipline honed to perfection by the demands of celebrity, I sometimes wondered if she intended to torture me. Then one day, as I passed her on the stairs, she grabbed my arm and said gaily, "I've been wanting to finish our conversation." I waited, feeling both alarm and excitement. "You must always wear shoes the same color as your hose," she said. "It means everything. It has been my secret for years," and she continued down the stairs, waving goodbye over the top of her beautiful head. There were other seemingly enigmatic, although sometimes helpful exhortations offered me over the days that we spent together. Sitting by the pool in Connie's garden early one evening, I mentioned that I was very hungry, particularly as dinner at Connie's was my only real food of the day and I could hardly wait for what I knew would be a delicious dinner. "Yes," said Audrey with a contented sigh. "I haven't had to think about beef Wellington in *weeks*."

That summer, too, the French model and actress Capucine lived at Connie's house while she secretly visited her lover, the producer Charlie Feldman, who was dying in a nearby hospital. His former wife, Jean Howard, disliked Capucine. John Dunne told me that Jean, who had been a Ziegfeld showgirl and actress in the Thirties and the girlfriend of Marlene Dietrich, had published a very good book of photographs she'd taken over the years, one of which, oddly enough, was of a man I would one day marry. Jean had given instructions that Capucine was not to be admitted to Feldman's hospital room, requiring Capucine to visit him in various elaborate disguises. One of the few times that Connie was angry with me was when I asked if the rumor that Capucine had once been a bellboy at the George V hotel in Paris was true. I was showing off that I was sophisticated enough not to mind if Capucine had once been a man, but Connie was not falling for it. "You still have an awful lot to learn, girl," she said as she left the room. I was mortified. I thought I'd been a very good student, learning as fast as I could certain invaluable social skills like cynicism and skepticism, as well as a number of survival techniques useful to women, but she caused me to wonder if perhaps I was learning the right things. It was then that I began to keep a notebook, mottled black and white like a child's copybook, writing bits and pieces in it when I came home at night, a form of conversation, but one in which I could tell the truth. I understood that Capucine's attempts at disguise and Audrey Hepburn's advice were humorous, at least to me, but not necessarily amusing to anyone else.

We were all happy to be at Connie's dinners, practicing a harmless sociability, despite the occasional indifference that the famous or the once-famous or the soon-to-be famous felt for those who were not famous and never would be famous. It was assumed that despite the occasional spark of individuality, we mostly had the same ambitions, the same conservative political views, the same ideals. It was a world in which it was everyone's business to please. This supposedly shared turn of mind allowed me to conceal myself as I sensed that it would be dangerous to do otherwise. Not unlike Ale, Connie was wary of anything that lay beneath the surface, her own or anyone else's surface. Remorse and guilt, my particular vocations, held no interest for her, perhaps because she found them to be especially wasteful exercises.

As much as I thought about other people, I did not want

them to think too much about me. I was self-invented, as were many of them, adapting myself minute by minute, a girl on the run. And yes, built for speed. My apartness and their sense that I was an outsider seemed to favor me. I rarely talked about myself, which I'd early discovered was an asset, and I wasn't easily shocked. That seemed to be enough to ensure my acceptance.

WITHIN A FEW MONTHS, Connie arranged for me to move from my apartment on Charleville into one of the three bungalows on Wilshire Boulevard owned by the interior decorator Gladys Belzer, who, Connie told me, was the mother of Loretta Young. The two-story bungalows, rented only to friends of Mrs. Belzer's, were hidden in a garden of gardenia and jasmine so dense that Wilshire Boulevard could not be seen or heard. My cottage, once the pied-à-terre of both Audrey Hepburn and Frank Sinatra, had a small brick courtyard and a fireplace. I arrived with a few pieces of furniture and five cartons of books, and Robby came with me.

Soon after I moved, I discovered that I'd lost my model's portfolio of photographs. Perhaps it had been stolen from my car, which I never locked, or perhaps I had left it in a photographer's studio, although in that instance it would have been returned to me. Images that had appeared as editorial pages in fashion magazines or in catalogues and newspapers were in the book, as well as many photographs. I did not try to find it, allowing myself to believe that it was mischance rather than intention. Nina Blanchard, the head of my agency, was furious when I told her, and said that a book was not an easy thing to lose, given its size and weight and, not least of all, its importance—logic that I was willing to follow until she added the word "importance," as it had always seemed to me that important things were just what I managed to lose. "You're going to be big!" she shouted. "Don't mess it up." To make a new book, as she suggested I do, would take time, but it could be done. Instead, I went to bed, and stayed there.

I read from the time that I woke in the morning until six o'clock each evening, when it was time to bathe and dress for dinner with Connie. When I closed the cover of one book, I would reach over the side of the bed, find another book from one of the piles on the floor, and start reading again. I read everything from *The Origins of Totalitarianism* to *W. C. Fields and Me*, rarely speaking and hardly moving. Now and then, I wondered if I was having a long overdue breakdown. Or if, having again found a refuge, I had succumbed to the grief that had haunted me since childhood. I had no answers, not that I tried very hard to find them. As I had done before, I lost myself in books.

When I had not felt strong enough as a child to go to school or, more likely, wanted to keep an eye on my mother and so pretended to be sick, I was allowed to spend the day at home on a daybed in the library, books in my lap—*The New Yorker 1950–1955 Album*, which was an anthology of cartoons; *Audubon's Birds of America*; *Currier and Ives' America*; several issues of my father's *American Heritage* hardback history magazines; and three small, square Skira illustrated studies of Manet, El Greco, and Toulouse-Lautrec. Given the frequency of my malingering, I knew the books by heart. That I did not understand much of what I read was not, and never would be, an impediment.

Once a week, my mother and I would drive in her blue Chevrolet convertible to the public library downtown, where we borrowed six books each, the maximum allowed. Like most children, I began with fairy tales, then myths and an abridged Homer, and Lewis Carroll. I was particularly entranced by a book entitled *A Child's History of the World*, which I mistakenly thought was a history of children when I first borrowed it. I would begin to read in the car on the way home. I was obsessively thorough, reading, for example, everything that I could find about pirates, going so far as to make with great care maps of sunken ships and the lonely beaches where caskets filled with gold and jewels were buried. I would singe the edges of a map with a match until it was sufficiently discolored for my liking. For a while, I read every book I could find about Indians as well as animals, including Conrad Richter's *The Light in the Forest*, the story of a boy who is held captive by Indians, and *The Yearling*, and Henry Williamson's *Tarka the Otter* and *Salar the Salmon*, books which left me in despair. My fascination with Egypt led me to spend weeks trying to make papyrus, cutting reeds with my rusty pen knife. It was more like sawing, and it took days, causing my hands to bleed, which at least taught me that reeds are quite difficult to cut.

My mother, who often read through the night, would come to my room after I'd gone to bed to make sure that I wasn't reading by flashlight under the covers or in the closet, a habit which she discouraged on grounds of health rather than any fear of my compulsions. She was unusually tolerant of a child's eccentricities, and solicitous of the innocence of others, perhaps because her own innocence had slipped away from her.

Certain of my childhood misapprehensions were the result of reading books that were too old for me, as well as overhearing misleading bits of conversation. As a girl, I was thrilled to possess the information that a woman's private parts were called a cud, despite my initial confusion as to what it was exactly that cows did with cud, and was even more bewildered when I looked up the word and found that it could also mean to talk things over, as in chewing the cud. My grandmother told me that a girl would die instantaneously if she had sexual intercourse before her first menstrual period, and the news that untimely intercourse could result in death became the foundation of my expanding collection of sexual facts. My next-door neighbor confided that she had learned from her family's Portuguese maid that during intercourse the man's testicles as well as his penis were stuffed, somewhat painfully for both, inside the vagina, which had a certain logic to it.

I'd raced feverishly through the otherwise imponderable book *Sex in History* by Reay Tannahill, stolen from the Honolulu Book Store, in which I learned about favored positions for intercourse, in particular one called "Hovering Butterflies," which I imagined required the rapid flapping of arms by both partners. I also decided that zoophilia referred to any sexual intercourse taking place in a zoo. I discovered Ovid's *The Art of Love* among my father's books and was quite surprised to read that men could greatly impress women by weeping. If they were unable to cry as needed, they were to douse their eyes with water. While I was already aware that there should be no "shocking goat" in a woman's armpits, a pleasing image all the same, the suggestion that an ill-shaped foot should be hidden in a boot of snow-white leather was news to me. Some of Ovid's tips proved in the end to be helpful. He warns that men who spend too much time arranging their locks should be avoided, and that still seems like wise advice, as does his stricture against piercing the arms of your hairdresser with pins. Not long after my discovery of Ovid, I happened upon Robert Van Gulik's detective novels about Judge Dee, based on an eighteenth-century Chinese detective named Dee Goong An. The Judge Dee books had an unsettling hint of sexual aberrance, often of a sadistic nature, and when I wrote a book report on Judge Dee in seventh grade, I discovered that Dr. Van Gulik had published a collection of erotic prints from the Ming dynasty which, to my disappointment, I was not allowed to borrow from the library, or even to see.

Although like most children I eventually learned to distinguish the more elaborate myths from what I believed was the no less distressing truth, what little I knew about sex was wildly inaccurate, if not fantastical, and cost me years of sexual pleasure. Later as an adolescent, when I was reading Hardy, the Brontës, Tennessee Williams, Tolstoy, George Eliot, and Faulkner, among others, it did not in any way strike me that these books might present an outdated or incomplete or even metaphorical picture of what I could expect to find once I left my isolated island in the North Pacific. I read French novels, but with less interest, as the main characters, other than Emma Bovary, tend to be young men in love with older women. I read poetry, mainly Dickinson and Eliot, but also Ginsberg, as my ninth-grade English teacher gave me a minuscule black-and-white pamphlet entitled *Howl*. It contained the poem "America," which thrillingly began with the words "Go fuck yourself with your atom bomb." I kept a notebook of my own very bad poems, full of longing, which I later gave to my grandmother, who kept it for years on the radiator that held the statue of the Infant of Prague. As an impediment rather than a stimulus to intellectual growth, the books that I read instilled in me an inchoate disaffection for the modern world, which took me rather too long to rectify.

When I first read *The Sun Also Rises*, I thought that Jake Barnes's impotence meant that he was ineffectual, in that he had a hard time getting a table in a restaurant, a definition which was not altogether inaccurate. I missed the important detail that Boy Fenwick in *The Green Hat* jumps out of a window on his wedding night because he has syphilis, not because Iris March is revealed to be unchaste, an error that led me to believe that a woman's sexual indiscretion before marriage could, if discovered, precipitate the sudden death of her anguished groom. I was completely baffled by *Sanctuary*, and had no idea that Temple Drake is raped by Popeye with a corn cob. Thanks to *The Alexandria Quartet*, one melodramatic passage in those shockingly bad books remained with me for years—Justine and her friend Clea, driving along the Alexandrian coast, stop to pick up a small cardboard box left by the side of the road. Inside the box is a perfectly formed dead baby, wrapped in newspaper. They are in a hurry, as Justine is giving a party, and when they arrive at her house, she stuffs the box into the drawer of a hall chest. The party, Clea later writes in her journal, was a great success.

In no time at all, I came to see myself as a heroine not unlike two of my favorite characters, Maggie Tulliver and Eustacia Vye. I flattered myself that I was like them—dark-haired, impetuous, full of head-tossing spirit and pride, and able to walk miles across open country, preferably in a cape. At the same time, I was in love with Faulkner's lawyer Gavin Stevens and with Trollope's Irishman, Phineas Finn. That both Maggie Tulliver and Eustacia Vye drown only deepened the myth that I was creating of and for myself. If I was superior to self-pity, I was also superior to consolation.

Among my reading in Mrs. Belzer's cottage was Auden's commonplace journal, and I began a second notebook in which I wrote certain words and passages that I found in books. This description in Chateaubriand was one of the first excerpts that I copied into the notebook: ". . . long-haired peasants in goat-skin tunics driving gaunt oxen along with shrill cries or walking behind heavy ploughs, like fauns tilling the soil." It was the fauns tilling the soil that particularly delighted me. And from Colette: "Is there any sleeping person you can be entirely sure you have not misjudged?" Or from *Jacob's Room*: "His slippers were incredibly shabby, like boats burned to the water's rim." And this from Lord Berners, which made me laugh: "She was an orphan, a condition which, for one reason and another, seems to incite sympathy."

If these entries thrilled me, it soon became apparent that there was a certain theme to other less exhilarating passages. "I request you to be patient and to keep a firm hold." That is Saul Bellow. "I must change. I must not live in the past, it will ruin me." Elizabeth Bowen. "His mistake was in assuming a limitation to female ruthlessness." Faulkner. And from the Gautier diaries: "I am very strong . . . and what is more, my metaphors make sense. That is what counts." I liked to think that each of them had been written for me.

As I was in many ways still a girl, reading enabled me to retain my childhood belief, at least for a little while, that the story and the world were equally real. I continued to find comfort in the mistaken idea that if I could only understand all that was happening around me, if I were assiduous and disciplined in my way, I would one day find clarity and even solace. If I could maintain the fragile, precarious balance inside, I might begin to mend. So far, however, my patient study of all that perplexed me in human behavior had not gained me much. I had yet to accept that most things, and especially my mother and her death, would always remain mysterious to me, and that in the end, it would be my experience of that mystery that was of interest. My sense of dislocation, my homesickness, my ceaseless longing for my mother seemed an inevitable affliction. The grief which always lay in wait for me had become, with little effort, my master.

Other than the guests at Connie's dinners, or Connie and Robby when we had dinner alone, there was no one to whom I spoke during the day. After six months of fairly peaceful torpor, I found myself waiting for the nice man from Jurgensen's who delivered the orange juice and pint containers of chicken salad that I ordered every few days. If I arrived early at Connie's, I would wander into the kitchen, where I would quiz Theodore, who was busy wiping glasses and opening bottles of wine, as to the night's menu, in which he took not the slightest interest. If Theodore was too distracted, I cornered Fortunato, whose responsibilities at dinner parties were limited to washing lettuce, to talk about Ferdinand Marcos. I was a bit desperate.

My lassitude had begun to wear on me and I was bored, mainly with myself. I decided that it was time to pull myself together, and I began to venture into Beverly Hills on small errands.

Although I was not working and had spent my savings, I needed almost no money. The lease on my car had understandably been canceled, and it had been taken away by the leasing company. Robby, tactfully and without complaint, paid the rent and the bill at Jurgensen's and at Hunter's Books. A few weeks before my twenty-third birthday, Connie told me that her gifts to me would be in honor of my new California life. As she was not aware that I read all day only to emerge in the evening when Robby drove us to her house for dinner, she was worried that I was housebound without a car. If I found a car to my liking, it would be one of my presents. I did not want her to buy me a car and told her that I rarely left the house, but she did not believe me and asked each time that I saw her, which was almost every day, if I had yet found a car. In the end, I chose an Opel, a tiny car so fragile that it seemed to be made of tinfoil, as it was the cheapest new car that I could find, costing only a thousand dollars. As for my other presents, she took me to meet her banker at City National Bank in Beverly Hills, where she gave me one hundred dollars to start a savings account, and she arranged for me to visit her gynecologist, Dr. Red Krohn, the doctor who had delivered her sons and almost every other child born in Beverly Hills in the previous forty years.

I went to see Dr. Krohn as directed and was put in an examining room, where I undressed and lay on a leather table, my feet in the cold metal stirrups, a white paper sheet covering me from my waist to my ankles. Dr. Krohn came into the room alone. He was wearing a black cowboy shirt with pearlized buttons and a turquoise and silver bolo. Once he sat on his little wheeled stool I could see only the top of his head with its thin strands of bright orange hair. The examination began. I knew what to expect as it was not my first visit to a gynecologist and I felt at ease, thanks to Connie's devotion to Dr. Krohn and, oddly enough, his costume. "You are looking marvelous!" he said, slightly surprised. I could hear the sound made by the speculum as it landed in a metal bowl and the snap of his gloves as he pulled them from his hands. As he pressed my lower abdomen, right and left, he said, "I'm counting the days to Acapulco, kiddo. Señor Pagliai promises me a marlin this time. Let me know when you and Bruno plan to leave and I'll fly down with you." He gave my knee a squeeze and was gone. I lowered my legs and slid forward to rest against the edge of the examining table. What just happened? I wondered. It was a bit worrying. And then I realized that Dr. Krohn had mistaken me, or rather a part of me, for the actress Merle Oberon, who was at least sixty years old. My vagina suddenly had its own provenance. Not bad, I said to myself.

I felt compelled to use the shiny little car that Connie had given me, if only to justify her generosity and to ease my guilt at accepting a present I didn't feel I deserved. I'd been told there was a riding academy at Point Dume, just off the Pacific Coast Highway, said to be owned by a rich German count, where one could hire thoroughbred horses for ten dollars a day. I drove there one hot morning, and soon was riding in the dusty canyons behind his ranch with a handful of children, mostly girls, twice a week. It is true that Egon von Merz was a count, and German, and that he had taught Elizabeth Taylor to ride for *National Velvet*, but he was not rich. Some of the tack was held together with large safety pins and rusty clamps. The stables were dilapidated and untidy, and the horses were not thorough-bred, although Egon assured me that many of them had only recently retired from show business, most notably an elderly horse that had been ridden by Pancho in *The Cisco Kid*. When Egon soon allowed me to ride alone, the thought of spending the day with a book or two began to seem less compelling. Brushwood jumps had been set along a dry creek bed, and there was the scent of sage, and acacia trees with their fragrant yellow flowers, and the buckeye tree, its silver bark reflecting the white winter light. The dusty odor of a worn library book, its binding held with glue, a smell that had seeped into me, now mingled with that of the bay laurel, the datura, and the lovely yerba mansa.

EIGHT

John Dunne was the first person, after my AP English teacher at Punahou, to encourage me to write. He knew that I had written stories and plays as a child, and suggested that I should do so again. He liked that I was keeping a notebook, and urged me to find a subject that interested me, or one that I thought would interest others, and write about it. He said that since I seemed unsure of myself, I should begin with journalism.

I wondered if I could write about Rodney Bingenheimer, the self-appointed Mayor of the Sunset Strip, whom I had read about in the *Free Press*. Rodney was a slight, soft-spoken boy of an ingenuous sweetness who had so ingrained himself in the music scene then developing that he himself would soon be famous. A few years earlier, when he was sixteen, his mother had driven him to Hollywood from their home in Mountain View and with the help of a guide to the homes of the stars, dropped him outside Connie Stevens's house with instructions to get her autograph. She had promptly driven away and he had not seen her since.

I found Rodney on the Strip, promenading in a large hat, and he agreed to let me interview him. I followed him on his rounds, responsibly carrying a reporter's steno pad and extra ballpoint pens. He introduced me to the Plaster Casters, among other hippie entrepreneurs, who had gained some notoriety for casting in plaster the erect penises of a number of musicians and actors. Rodney took me with him to watch the Plaster Casters, two young women who had been friends since high school, working in shifts to give Anthony Newley an erection in the hope of jamming his stiff penis into a lump of wet plaster. I did not stay to see if they succeeded, but Rodney later assured me that their hard work had resulted in a sculpture which, according to Newley, belonged in a museum. Later, Rodney became an intimate of Sonny and Cher, and a favorite friend of David Bowie. It seems that his many otherwise inexplicable sexual conquests of young girls had been conducted as auditions on behalf of the musicians and roadies who cultivated him, and explains to some degree his friendships with them.

Once I had arranged and then arranged again my notes into a vaguely coherent story, John Dunne helped me to edit it. We sat on the floor of Mrs. Belzer's cottage as he crossed out paragraphs and corrected my grammar. I was very grateful, and did everything that he suggested I do. He wanted me to submit it to *Rolling Stone*, but I knew that it was not good enough, even with the many improvements he'd made to it. He was my first editor. Despite his frequent reminders that I should be working on a story, any story, I did not write anything more.

After the riots in South Central Los Angeles in 1965, Budd Schulberg, a writer whom I'd met at one of Connie's parties, founded the Watts Writers Workshop, a collective of poets, writers, and artists, where classes in art and painting, and tutoring in math and English, were held for neighborhood children. I wrote to Schulberg to ask if I could volunteer as an after-school tutor, and I began to work there two days a week. Although I understood that my contribution was so glancing as to be almost meaningless, I spent every Tuesday and Thursday afternoon helping a handful of fifth-grade children with their homework. They were without judgment or fear and full of affection, and I was soon very attached to them. In April, when Dr. King was killed, I squeezed my class into the Opel and drove across town to Manhattan Beach—which was against the rules, volunteers were not allowed to see the children away from the Workshop—where we stood in shallow water, hands linked, as some of them could not swim, and I told them that Dr. King was dead.

I sometimes felt that I was deceiving them when I preached that learning to read and to add figures would make all the difference in the world. Orwell writes that despite Dickens's obvious condemnation of Victorian England in his novels, he did not go so far as to advocate a change in the system, or believe in the possibility of social reform through government or institutions, but hoped instead for small moments of justice. Even if there were reform, Dickens did not think it would make much of a difference. His contempt was not for society, but for human nature, and I sometimes felt the same.

I was as wary of the black power movement as I was of hippies, especially after it was said that Huey Newton's goals were, in order of importance, to close down Howard University, to liberate Washington, and to seize and occupy the White House. If his plan was meant as metaphor or simply as theater, I understood that, but I otherwise failed to see its efficacy. Perhaps I was suffering from a lack of irony. It would not make any difference to the children at the Workshop, who were hemmed in at every point, subject to endless disappointment and injustice, if not violence. Aside from the Workshop itself and other volunteer enterprises, the riots had not resulted in any beneficial changes in their lives or the lives of their parents. They would not be helped by fantasies of revenge, or by the expectation that an imminent armed uprising would free them, after the necessary bloodshed, once and for all. I was already suspicious of the need to exercise power over others, no matter who they might be. Incendiary and coercive speechifying seemed irresponsible at best, and delusional at worst. It also seemed to confirm the anxieties and fears of white racists, which, in the hope of provoking violence, may have been Newton's intention.

While at the Workshop, I'd noticed a black man who taught painting to some of the older children. His name was Bernie Casey. He soon made it clear that he had no desire to know me, which increased my interest in him, and I found myself inventing ways to get his attention, usually by asking a question. Did he know where the crayons might be? The fire extinguisher? I discovered from another volunteer that he was a halfback with the Rams, and revered in Los Angeles for catching the winning touchdown pass during the last thirty seconds of a 1967 end-of-season game against the Packers. He was also a

The football player, painter, and actor Bernie Casey,
Los Angeles, 1969

painter, making bright canvases on which he inscribed verses
of his poetry. That he was a football player as well as a poet and
an artist seemed to unnerve people. Sensing a certain skepticism that he could possibly be good in all three disparate ways,

especially given his color, he once said to a prospective donor who was making a tour of the Workshop, "You know, a man can be a deep-sea diver and also make china."

It was, he later told me, my friendship with my students that at last gained his attention, rather than my irritating questions. As I was still living with Robby, I began to visit him at his house in the Hollywood Hills, usually after a class at the Workshop. I felt no compunction in lying to Robby, who had become a friend rather than a lover, although I sometimes wondered if he preferred the time when I used to read all day, as he at least knew where I was and what I was doing, but he never questioned me. During football season, if I saw Bernie on a Monday after a game, he would be in pain, his arms and legs and back covered with contusions and bruises. He once asked if I had ever been pregnant, which made me wonder if he found me insufficiently desirable. Or, equally distressing, that my vagina after only three partners was stretched to enormity. It was not what he meant, of course, but I was too unsure of myself to see that he may have been asking in a subtle way if I used birth control. I was naturally modest, and it was difficult for me to undress before him, especially as his rooms were full of light. As embarrassed as I was at the thought of my possible deformity, I was more embarrassed to ask him to close the curtains lest he think me not cool. I removed my clothes in an elaborate, complicated dance so as never to appear completely naked, a performance which must have baffled or, worse, bored him. It did not occur to me to ask him why he wondered if I had been pregnant. I simply assumed that I was misshapen in some way that I had not yet considered.

The difference in our color was always there between us,

not as a provocation to erotic arousal but as the thing that separated and would always separate us. He seemed more aware of
my whiteness than I was of his blackness, although I was sometimes struck by a sudden glimpse of my pale hand upon his
back. He liked to position my feet next to his own, a contrast
that made him laugh, and not only because of the difference
in size. Years later, I was to sense a similar feeling of unease
when I lived in Berlin, where an awareness of the crimes of
the past, an evil that had not fully been resolved, was always
present. The German friends that I made were unable to keep
from mentioning the war, often upon first meeting, perhaps in
the hope of lessening the weight of their inherited guilt. The
difference, of course, is that for Bernie, it was I who had inherited a shameful past.

In the summer of 1969, Robby and Richard Roth rented a
house in the Malibu Colony, a long drive from Beverly Hills,
but with houses more substantial and much larger than the rickety structures on the Pacific Coast Highway, cantilevered on
redwood beams that shuddered with each incoming tide and
passing truck. The Colony had a barred gate and a guardhouse,
with one narrow road running parallel to the beach. People
who lived year-round in the Colony, as opposed to renters, liked
to boast of the numbers on their prescriptions, filled by the
tiny Malibu pharmacy, as proof of their superior discernment,
at least in regard to real estate, which taught me that one can
be snobbish about almost anything. The screenwriter Tom
Mankiewicz proudly displayed a pill bottle with a prescription
that bore the number two, which afforded him an unquestioned
distinction.

Two years earlier, my brother Rick and my sister Tina had

taken refuge in our grandmother's house in Philadelphia, leaving behind in Honolulu our brother Michael, who was then fourteen, and our sister Anne, who was ten years old. Rick had been admitted to Villanova and Tina had found work downtown selling books in Gimbels department store. I borrowed money from Robby to send each of them a plane ticket, and they spent a month with me that summer. They, too, had yet to recover from childhood, particularly the cruelties of our stepmother, which had been directed most viciously at Tina, whose stoicism had spurred our stepmother to torments of an unusually sadistic ingenuity. Rick was reserved and cautious, in contrast to Tina's need to speak her mind.

At night, my brother and sister and I would sit in the garden where there was the smell of the ocean and the vaguely sickening scent of ylang-ylang, reminding us of Gertrude's boyfriend Benjie. We talked about the past in a tentative, elliptical way, fearful of causing one another too much distress. When they asked, "How could you have left us?" I had no answer for them. Once in the darkness, I heard my brother gasp in an attempt not to cry. When I reached to touch him, he pushed away my hand.

When we could not bear to talk any longer, we studied the constellations with the help of a flashlight and H. A. Rey's book *The Stars*. If I felt a certain frustration whenever I was compelled by circumstance, or by choice, to experience beauty on my own, causing it to appear less real if there was no one to share it with me, it was thrilling to sit in the dark with my brother and sister, now and then pointing to a star. We knew that we would soon be separated, but we were tranquil, even peaceable, and full of forgiveness as we listened to what we once had called the Music of the Spheres.

Robby was in town during the day, as was Richard, who was an assistant to the French director Jacques Demy, who was making a film called *The Model Shop*. Richard was more sophisticated than Robby and his friends, most of whom Robby had known since they were boys at school in Beverly Hills. Richard had lived in London, which greatly impressed me. His discernment and tact helped to keep me steady, especially after my brother and sister returned to Philadelphia.

The aggressively amiable television actor Larry Hagman and his Swedish wife, Mai, were the king and queen of the Colony, holding court a few houses away, Larry sitting in a sarong at the edge of his hot tub, allowing one a peek at his genitals as he smoked a joint. Once a day, he would put on a caftan to lead a disorderly band of acolytes up and down the shoreline, some of them carrying Tibetan prayer flags and bottles of champagne.

The singer John Phillips stopped me one afternoon as I was walking on the beach to ask if I could teach him to swim, a question which I took seriously for a moment until I saw the saturnine smile which seemed to mock us both. He was staying at a house rented by his friend, the English pop star and movie director Michael Sarne, who was somewhat improbably making a film of Gore Vidal's book *Myra Breckenridge*, with Raquel Welch. Michael's wife, Tanya, and his father were also there that summer, as was Geneviève Waïte, a whimsical South African actress whom John later married. Michael's father, who was Czech, was my first experience of an Eastern European intellectual. Simply to say good morning to him provoked a dis-

sertation on Jan Masaryk, and I kept away from him. Although
the women were less forthcoming in expressing any views they
might have held, other than their belief in free love and drugs
for all, they were a bit intimidating in their casual amorality.
They took little notice of me, to my relief, in part because they
couldn't imagine that someone as straight as I appeared to be
and, in fact, was, might interest John. It was a surprise to me
as well.

I would walk to the Sarnes' house and if we were so fortunate as to find the others away, John, who was or was not
separated from his wife, Michelle, and I would spend an hour
or two in a bed increasingly littered with sand, cigarette papers, and the occasional amyl nitrate capsule. I once woke to
find his daughter Chynna, who was then a year and a half old
and who was spending the weekend with him, rummaging in
a large black leather Gladstone bag that he carried about with
him and kept next to his bed when he slept. The bag held every
possible drug and implement, most of which had been scattered across the floor by Chynna as she contentedly emptied
the bag. I woke John when I jumped out of bed to lift her from
the pile of drugs, and he asked if I couldn't be a little more
quiet, as he was trying to sleep. Chynna and I went for a walk
until her mother, who was four hours late, arrived to collect
her. I did not see John again, and although he called me a few
times, once to ask me the name of the opera in which a statue
begins to speak, it was an easy parting for both of us, perhaps
even a relief.

I was removed from the general air of youthful rebellion, in
part because I did not take drugs, but also because I was wary
of random rebellion and the zeal for indiscriminate personal

expression. I was often advised by hippie acquaintances as well as would-be seducers that any manifestation of will or desire was just fine, provided it did not hurt anyone, but I did not believe it. Life in a commune held no interest for me. I couldn't help but think that shared tasks in smoke-filled yurts, as well as shared sexual partners, would lead to a kind of tedium. I found irritating the assumption that farmers, or Native Americans, or gypsies dressed themselves in denim overalls or buckskin or bandanas hemmed with coins in order to make what was called a personal statement. I was irritated if someone said, "Well, he's always been nice to me," in regard to a person notably evil. The lack of irony upset me even more, but to object too strenuously was to appear bad-tempered and humorless. Perhaps irony is impossible in any seditious movement—even the Dadaists, of all people, needed a little irony. The idea that hundreds of people would assemble at the Pentagon in order to levitate it three feet off the ground, a gesture that I assumed was meant to be facetious as well as obstreperous, appealed to me, as long as I did not have to have a conversation with anyone who believed it really could be done if everyone only concentrated hard enough.

My mistrust of hippie philosophy had less to do with drugs or free love or a loathing of relativism than with my childhood experience of tending to a mother who was coming apart, a situation that required me to make quick and often irrevocable distinctions: this is bad, this is not too bad, this is all right, this is very, very bad. For me, the abandonment of these discriminations meant dissolution and possibly even death. How could I possibly have let down my vigilance? It was inconceivable. As tempted by abandon as I was occasionally, I would not in the end have been capable of it. Without an interpretive intelligence, I was lost.

That August, we heard what was at first thought to be a particularly frightening rumor that Sharon Tate and some of her friends had been murdered at Sharon and Roman Polanski's rented house on Cielo Drive in Beverly Hills. The murders were said to be extremely vicious, especially as Sharon was pregnant. The rumor implied that Roman somehow was responsible, perhaps because of the orgies said to have taken place at the house. Another rumor suggested that the real targets had been Candice Bergen and Terry Melcher, who were the previous tenants of the house. There had been many parties that year at Cielo Drive and I noticed that people's first reaction when they soon learned that the rumors were true was to say, "I might have been there!" which seemed yet another way to associate one's self with celebrity. I, too, had been to parties there, where to my surprise, I once saw a contemplative Danny Kaye, whom I would not have thought a likely companion to the men in their velvet jackets and poet's shirts and the barefoot girls dancing on the lawn, lying in a hammock with a banjo. John Dunne, when he called to tell me the news of the murders, said, "You can hear toilets flushing all over town," as people disposed of their drugs. Joan said that the murders marked the end of the Sixties in California. Although I was wary of such pronouncements, I immediately wrote it in my notebook.

At the end of the summer, I left Mrs. Belzer's cottage, and Robby, and Connie, my real beloved, and moved with a friend to a house in Beachwood Canyon said to have once been vandalized by Jim Morrison. I no longer had any use for Ale's beautiful clothes. I'd left some dresses and coats in Philadelphia with my grandmother, and the rest of Ale's clothes were in Connie's cedar closet in Beverly Hills. I had very few possessions, other than books. During the day, I wore miniskirts and bell-bottomed jeans and white long-sleeved T-shirts without slogans or advertising, and my Mexican huaraches from Acapulco. If I went out in the evening, a white broderie anglaise dress from Jax and red ballet slippers.

I no longer went to Connie's house every night. I saw her perhaps twice a week when she expected me for dinner. Robby, who had remained a friend, knew an agent at the William Morris Agency named Benny Thau who was looking to hire someone to read the books and scripts that Warren Beatty received as submissions, and Robby wondered if I might be interested in the job. I went to see Mr. Thau, a gnomish and tidy little man, who, Robby told me, had been Nancy Reagan's boyfriend before her marriage.

Mr. Thau asked me to meet with Warren Beatty at his penthouse at the Beverly Wilshire, a block from the agency. The screenwriter Robert Towne was with Warren when I arrived, as was Warren's secretary, Helen. Towne was wearing so much scent that I immediately had a headache. Warren, handsome, boyish, confident, began by telling me that I was too tan. I told him that I was from Hawai'i, as if that might explain my skin color, and he let it go at that. I said that I had not previously been employed as a script reader, or anything else, for that matter. I did not mention my brief reign as Miss Aluminum, or that I had been a model. Fortunately, he was not particularly interested in my work experience, but wanted to know who I knew in Hollywood. When I said that I knew the Dunnes, he smiled, and so did Robert Towne, who seemed to agree with Warren about everything. Warren then asked if he could see my legs. I was wearing a short linen skirt, and I placed my hands on my hips to raise it a few inches, not in the least offended as Warren and Bob checked out my legs. "Can you start tomorrow morning?" Warren asked.

Although I would not have called my work as a script reader a real job, it was hardly a hobby. Perhaps I would have regarded it as more serious work if I had an office or even a desk, but as it was I picked up the scripts and books that I was to read each week, leaving behind those that I had already read and reviewed. My salary was one hundred and fifty dollars a week, for which I wrote a synopsis of each submission and a short evaluation as to whether or not it might make an interesting film. Most actors and producers, as well as studios and talent agencies, engage script readers, and their reports, many of which I read, thanks to Benny Thau, who gave them to me surreptitiously as they were considered confidential, were often tedious and dull, as well as twelve to fifteen pages long. I wrote at most two pages of synopsis, and only a paragraph of evaluation. I never once read something that I thought would make a good movie. A script submitted anonymously rarely resulted in a film project. I had no illusions about the importance of my work. It was really just a way to neaten Warren's desk.

Warren would be on the telephone when I arrived, his calls first screened through the hotel switchboard or by his answering service. I noticed that sometimes when he took a call, he hurriedly did a few squats holding twenty-pound weights in each hand so that when he picked up the receiver he was out of breath. It took me a while to realize that he wanted the person on the phone, presumably but not certainly a girl, to think that he had been interrupted while making love. It must have been flattering to think that Warren Beatty considered you of sufficient importance to abandon, if only for a few minutes, his partner in bed. Although he was seeing Julie Christie, who would stay with him when she was in town, there were endless sexual encounters. He said that his romance with Julie only heightened his success with other women, as he immediately told anyone in whom he was interested that he was in love with Julie. This, of course, fascinated me. I did not think it was a ploy that would work with me, although I had yet to experience that kind of approach, and I wondered if I, too, might not find it an irresistible enticement, given its suggestion of inconsequence.

I once asked if he didn't occasionally tire of his insatiable need to seduce. He looked at me for a moment, gauging whether or not it was worth the effort to answer me truthfully, and then said, "It's simple. You get smacked a lot, but you also get fucked a lot." He was obsessed with Joan Dunne, not because she was becoming increasingly well-known and admired for her writing, but because she showed no interest in sleeping with him. He asked me to include him if I was having dinner with her and, if possible, to arrange that he sit next to her. When I told Joan that I would be pimping for him, she was amused, although not as much as John, who was titillated by the idea that Warren wanted to sleep with his wife.

Warren required that anyone who worked for him, or who was a friend like Bob Towne or a girl whom he was chasing or had chased or would someday chase, be in constant touch with him, which meant ten or twelve phone calls a day to him, often from a pay phone. There was no need for conversation, as all he wanted to know was what you were doing, where you had been, where you were going, and if you'd had sex with anyone since your last phone call. If I told him that I was having lunch with a male friend, he would want to know if I had slept with him or was planning on sleeping with him. He wanted to know where we were having lunch and what we were eating, and if anyone he knew was in the restaurant. These conversations would take only a few minutes, but they were exhausting, especially as I had little of interest to tell him. It occurred to me to make up stories for his amusement, a Beverly Hills Scheherazade, but I realized that it would only make things complicated, especially as I had been mindful to keep things as simple as possible.

Warren told me that he had learned many things from the producer Charlie Feldman, whom he idolized. As Feldman had always given gifts of expensive handbags to his conquests, Warren often sent me to the nearby Gucci store on Beverly Drive to choose presents to give to girls. I hadn't found the examination of my legs humiliating, but I didn't like shopping for him. As I came through the door, the sales clerks would quickly assemble numerous handbags on the glass display cases. As I used Warren's credit card, I explained after the first twenty-five purchases that the bags were not for me, and they soon had bags wrapped as gifts waiting for me when I came into the store.

My sister had come from Philadelphia to live with me, and was staying in a small apartment in the garage of the house in Beachwood Canyon. I saw Bernie Casey now and then, but he was not what could be called a real boyfriend. I would go to his house, as he never invited me to dinner in a restaurant or to a movie or for a walk on the beach at Venice, and I wondered if it was because I was a white girl.

I was often invited to parties by John and Joan at their two-story house on Franklin Avenue, a few blocks from the glass tower where Penny Brahms had rented an apartment. It was north of the Strip, where the houses were mostly rentals, their tenants changing monthly, if not weekly. The house sat directly on the street, with a cracked cement walkway leading from the narrow sidewalk to the front door. There was an overgrown garden, and a ruined tennis court, still bearing a torn and sagging net. It was said that the Dunnes' house had been the Japanese Consulate before Pearl Harbor, which only added to its mysterious charm. It was not a desirable neighborhood, although the houses were large and handsome, which may have been why the Dunnes lived there, especially as Joan was liable to a certain perversity. Given her particular character, based in part on a mistrust of the fashionable, the neighborhood suited her. She chose not to live in the center of things until much later, when John insisted, despite her wish to remain in her house in Brentwood, on moving to New York.

Although some of the same people whom I met at Connie's dinners would also be at the Dunnes', the mood was less predictable and less conservative. I no longer had to pretend to be fascinated, and I did not have to ignore the hand on my leg, or spell the word "ophthalmology." I could talk about the Vietnam War as much as I liked. And if someone tried to touch me under the table, I could shout, Hey! Watch it! or I could touch him, too. Any journalists or writers in town from New York or Europe would turn up at the Dunnes', along with Christopher Isherwood and Janis Joplin and Ed Ruscha and Linda

Ronstadt and Jerry Brown. I first met the costume designer and later director Joel Schumacher at the Dunnes' house. He was irresistible, his voice always on the verge of laughter. I sensed that nothing one could do would shock or alarm him. He also happened to be beautiful, and I was a little in love with him. One night, Joan overheard someone mention that drugs were available upstairs where her young daughter, Quintana, was sleeping. Running upstairs, she found some of her guests dispensing peyote in the hall outside the child's bedroom. When she asked them to leave, a musician who had come with Janis Joplin said, "You don't know what you're missing, babe," and Joan, following them down the stairs to the front door, said, "Yes, I do."

Ivan Moffat in the garden at
Outpost Drive, Los Angeles, 1975

It was at the Dunnes' that I began my long friendship with the English screenwriter Ivan Moffat, whose mother was the poet and actress Iris Tree. He was rarely without a cigarette, and his tie and jacket were often flecked with ash, his fingertips stained yellow with tobacco. He was sometimes so tiresomely at ease that I wondered if he made no distinction between one person and the next. Some people found him trying, perhaps because of his reliance on the anecdotal, which hindered a broader conversational exchange. He'd been one of the screenwriters on the film *Giant*, directed by George Stevens, and had worked with Stevens on his film *A Place in the Sun*, but he hadn't done very much since. He had been in the Second World War, serving under Stevens, who was the head of a Signal Corps unit charged with documenting war crimes. He was with Stevens when he entered the concentration camp at Dachau, shooting footage that was used as evidence at Nuremberg. Ivan once caught me lip-synching the story of his affair with Ricki Huston, Anjelica's mother, who he claimed had received him one night wearing nothing but a Navajo silver necklace. I had heard the story a number of times, as I had heard other stories, but I had a crush on him, and in that instance, I was jealous, not bored.

I met John's brother Dominick at Franklin Avenue. His first words to me were, "I'm a fool for fart jokes." We did not become close friends, perhaps because of the tempestuous relationship of the two brothers. John and Joan's nickname for Nick was Pepe, and it was not affectionate. I often saw Earl and Camilla McGrath at the Dunnes' house. They lived in the penthouse apartment at the Chateau Marmont before renting a house on Robertson Drive, a move considered quite daring, as

Robertson was still a commercial neighborhood. Camilla took photographs of her friends, which was not considered intrusive, although it was found to be irritating when Nick Dunne pulled out his camera. Earl, thought by some to be gay, was excessive, irreverent, unpredictable. He was a story editor at Twentieth Century Fox, surely a distracted and bored story editor. He was bereft of reasonable limitations, and many people disapproved of him. It was impossible to have a conversation with him of any gravity or depth. He told me that as a child in the small Wisconsin town where he lived he had made pocket money by drowning kittens at a dime apiece. Arriving late at a party in a nightclub for a movie star, he spotted John in a crowded banquette, squeezed against the guest of honor. Earl leaned across the table to shout, "I *knew* that's where I'd find you," causing John to throw his drink in his face. I was startled and Earl was startled, but no one else seemed to notice or, more likely, to care. Earl calmly wiped his face on his sleeve and pushed into the booth.

Earl and Camilla knew everyone in the very particular world that Ivan Moffat called Nescafé Society, an international set of amusing and ambitious hustlers, impoverished noblemen with ostentatiously good manners, would-be artists and writers, real artists and writers, louche social climbers, and the occasional banker in a chalk-striped suit. People from out of town would often arrive at the McGraths' with their suitcases, having come straight from the airport. Earl had once lived in New York with Barbara Skelton, the beautiful English wife of Cyril Connolly and then George Weidenfeld, and the girlfriend of men as varied as King Farouk and Robert Silvers. She was said to be the inspiration for the character Pamela Flitton in

Anthony Powell's *A Dance to the Music of Time*. I once asked Earl what it was about Skelton that made her irresistible to so many different men, apart from her beauty, and he said that she instantly intuited what it was that a man wanted from her, particularly what he wanted in the way of sex. That Earl, too, had been her lover only added to the mystery. Later he worked for the Rolling Stones and at Atlantic Records for Ahmet Ertegun, where his amorality and perverse sense of humor served him well.

As for drugs, there was a lot of marijuana and mushrooms and acid, and there was cocaine. As I was intent on keeping my brain from humming more urgently than I could manage, I used alcohol and the occasional quaalude to calm myself. One night, the writer Frank Conroy slipped me a tiny packet wrapped in tinfoil and told me to go to the bathroom with it. I did as I was told, but as I had no idea what was inside, I opened the packet upside down, causing the coke to fall into the toilet and onto my skirt. When I returned and slipped the empty packet into Frank's hand, he screamed at me in fury.

Joan asked me to stay in the Franklin Avenue house as she and John were going to Hawai'i. I'd been uneasy living in the hills, with their intimation of menace, and I was happy to have a place to live, at least for a little while, where I would not feel ill at ease. I moved into an upstairs bedroom crowded with file boxes and neat piles of personal papers, research, and manuscripts. A colony of rats lived in a palm tree just outside a window on the staircase landing, and each night I would race up the stairs to bed, convinced that they were waiting for me, their eyes red with reflected light. Joan had encouraged me to drive her yellow Corvette while they were away, although driving it was like mounting a wild animal. When I cautiously accelerated, the car lunged forward as if suddenly let free from its cage, and I did not use it often. It was not the kind of car you took to Ralphs Market on Doheny, or perhaps it was, and I didn't know better.

When the Dunnes returned from their trip, they suggested that I stay a little longer. I was relieved not to have to return to the house in Beachwood Canyon, and we settled into an easy routine in which I tried to keep out of their way. In the morning, Joan, wearing dark glasses, would come downstairs to drink a bottle of Coke she took from the refrigerator. She would be angry if one of the Cokes was missing, and the Mexican housekeeper and I were careful not to move the bottles from their place on the top shelf. She would then light a cigarette and open a can of salted almonds from one of the cases that her mother sent each Christmas from Sacramento. There was no conversation, the only sounds the snap of the aluminum tab and the whoosh of air as the can of nuts was opened. She would then return to her office on the second floor, where she would work until one o'clock, as did John in his own office, when they would meet for lunch prepared by the housekeeper or go to a restaurant. I found this so instructive, so efficient, and even so romantic in its way, that I wrote their schedule in my notebook, adding it to a rather short list I entitled "Tips for Domestic Contentment."

She was as fastidious, as particular in her domestic life, as she was in her writing, all effort concealed, not through any devious design, but because she was by nature secretive. She made certain domestic decisions (what food to serve at a dinner party, whom to invite) very quickly. Artichoke vinaigrette. An orange and endive salad. Mexican chicken—she was particularly irritated when Nora Ephron pestered her for the recipe—and for dessert, big strawberries with their stems, eaten with brown sugar and sour cream. Cinnamon in the coffee.

Despite the eccentricity of the household, there was love between them, and respect. She was also afraid of him, given the violence of his temper. I soon grew accustomed to his easy superiority of manner, made bearable by his quick intelligence and his willingness to laugh, although I, too, always kept in mind his volatility, which was unpredictable and often irrational. He liked to boast that he never took sides in a divorce, and I would wonder, Why not? You take sides in everything else. I was so lacking in calculation, always a bit of a handicap, that I didn't at first realize that his ostentatious neutrality in the matter of divorce was shrewdness on his part, given his social ambition. One night at dinner in a restaurant, he was infuriated when I said that I'd heard that Jann Wenner was gay. He slammed down his glass of Scotch, shouting that he had never heard such malicious gossip, and left the table to recover himself in the men's room. I was so unnerved, so angry myself, that I rose to leave, but Joan grabbed my arm and begged me to stay, making me promise that I would not leave her alone with him.

People were disappointed, if not disbelieving, to discover that Joan was not a liberal. Although she did not hide her admiration for Barry Goldwater and John Wayne, she was also crazy about Jerry Brown. She mistrusted partisanship, believing that one's adherence to a particular ideology not only did not matter in the end, but that it could be dangerous. She was by nature averse to orthodoxy, especially when it was political and enforced by popular thought. She was a conservative in an old landed-gentry way, as might be expected of a fifth generation

Joan Didion and John Gregory Dunne in their house at
Trancas Beach, Los Angeles, 1971

descendant of Protestant pioneers who had refused to accompany their wagon train through the Donner Pass, a sensible decision as it turned out, as those travelers who survived the Donner Pass did so by eating their companions. She was not a contrarian, which would have made her exhausting, although refusal had been a part of her nature since childhood. She once told me that the first time she stopped eating was when her father went away to war.

LATER THAT YEAR, I met the production designer Paul Sylbert and his wife, Anthea, who was a costume designer. She was charming, quick, and impenetrable, sophisticated in a way that I had not yet encountered, despite the Dunnes' parties, and I was unsettled by her. She seemed instinctively to know too much about me. Later, I was relieved and comforted by this, grateful that I did not have to explain myself to her. I never saw her in anything but well-cut trousers, her black hair reaching to her chin, a cigarette and sometimes a cigar between her fingers. She was attractive to men, and was said to have love affairs, which interested me.

She was often away on location, when I would meet Paul for dinner. He was learning to play the Bach cello sonatas on a guitar and he invited me to stop by his house one evening to hear him play. As I sat there, a man walked through the living room to the kitchen, moving quietly so as not to disturb us. I knew that Paul had an identical twin brother named Richard, and Paul explained that Dick was staying with him while he recovered from hepatitis, contracted in Mexico while work-ing with Mike Nichols on *Catch 22*. I took one quick look at Dick and thought to myself that he was the man for whom I'd been waiting. He was very handsome, more handsome than his brother, and tall and thin, with pale blue eyes. My first thought was that he was too dashing to be reliable.

Dick Sylbert on the set, 1965

The two were production designers, and to make things a bit odder, they dressed alike and both smoked a pipe. That night they each wore what I later discovered was their daily outfit—a long-sleeved khaki shirt, white cotton undershirt, khaki trousers, brown leather loafers, white cotton socks, and a polka-dot cotton scarf tied at the neck. I thought, Oh, they're dandies.

In the following weeks, I began to see Dick around town, once at the Aware Inn on Sunset Boulevard, where I often went to dinner with Richard Roth or the Dunnes. One night I saw him at a party at Earl and Camilla McGrath's house. I sat on the floor next to him, and by the end of the evening, he asked me to dinner. On one of our first dates, he told me that when he and Paul were sixteen, they would fight each night in their bedroom, darting around their beds, silent so as not to alert their mother as they tried to suffocate each other without leaving a mark. They fought until one of them fell to the floor, struggling to breathe. I wondered why he had told me this, and if he was asking me to choose between them. If that were so, I was surprised that he did not know that I had already made my choice. There had never been a question as to who it would be.

I left Franklin Avenue and moved back to the house in Beachwood Canyon. One afternoon, I broke a date with Bernie Casey, telling him that I had to meet a friend, which was mildly the truth, as Dick had called to ask if he could see me. I was reading on my bed when Bernie appeared at the screen door leading from my room to the garden and put his fist through the screen. He was dressed in a fringed leather vest with no shirt, which seemed both threatening and stylish. I had no idea that he knew where I lived. I was surprised by his anger, as I knew that he saw women other than me and I did not consider that I meant more to him than any of the others. And perhaps I didn't. I was not so much frightened as embarrassed that I'd been caught in a lie, and I went to the door to apologize. He did not say a word, just stared at me for a moment, and turned away. I never saw him again.

NINE

I was twenty-four years old and Dick was forty-two. Because of the hepatitis he had contracted in Mexico, he did not drink, so I did not drink, either. Under his discriminating tutelage, I continued my education in literature, music, and art. After service in the Korean War, Dick and Paul had attended the Tyler School of Art at Temple University in Philadelphia. Several of his fellow students were to remain his friends throughout his life, including the artists David Levine and Aaron Shikler, the art dealer Roy Davis, and the painter and frame maker Robert Kulick. Like Dick, they were not interested in contemporary art. He encouraged me instead to look hard at three of his favorite painters, Manet, Eakins, and Velasquez. He asked me to study the Velasquez portrait of Philip IV. "Do you see it?"

he asked excitedly, the smoke from his pipe swirling around his head. "The entire history of Western art can be found in the triangle between the king's arm, his baton, and the edge of his coat." I didn't see it, but I did not tell him that. I adored him, taking in all that he said. I wanted him to find me a quick and grateful student, but I was also a little afraid of him, having seen how dismissive he could be, and sometimes even unkind. He was seldom wrong about things, except when his impatience prevented him from a modesty and even humility that would only have illuminated his brilliance.

While listening to him, I sometimes tried to remember what it was that I had learned from my father, but other than cribbage, chess, and betrayal, there was not much else. Although my mother read good books, that is, not bestsellers or romances, she preferred Strauss waltzes and melodic orchestral pieces like Ponchielli's "Dance of the Hours," which I once used as music in a play that I wrote and directed when I was ten, forcing my brothers and sisters to be fairies and flowers ("Flower of the ages, bid you tell, your name, your age, and where you dwell"). She listened to *Swan Lake*, and the occasional military march, but she was not interested in classical music other than the more obliging pieces of Chopin and Schumann. What she loved most was the music of Artie Shaw and Benny Goodman, the dance music of her adolescence, and I loved it, too. Her interest in art was limited to the Impressionists, while my father admired Bernard Buffet. Is it any wonder that I read and looked at everything Dick suggested, much to my edification and, more, to my delight? I studied Dick, too, so intently that I wondered if he was the first man I'd ever really noticed.

I liked that we read many of the same books and looked at

the same things, although his knowledge was far deeper than my own. What is more, like me, he read during the day, a habit that is less common than one imagines, especially as many people think of reading as a hobby, or worse, as an inducement to sleep. He gave me the book *Technicians of the Sacred*, an anthology of traditional chants, spells, and incantations, where I found a vision song of the Gitksan Indians that I wrote in my commonplace book: "beehives were stinging my body or the ghosts of bees, giants & the old woman working me until I grew . . . hurt me in dreams, in my head." It reminded me of my nightmares.

While I still raced through the work of one writer before moving on to the next, I particularly loved Faulkner and was never without one of his books, reading some of them two and three times a year. I had recently discovered Pepys's diaries and the twelve volumes of Casanova's memoirs and was thinking about reading *Genji* again when Dick hinted that I might like to read something a bit more modern, writers who were less familiar to me like Céline and Flann O'Brien and Beckett. At his suggestion, I also read history—*Akenfield*, *Wisconsin Death Trip*, *Cortés and Montezuma*, and Paul Fussell's *The Great War and Modern Memory*. He gave me the Gluck opera *Orfeo ed Euridice*, and Saint-Saëns's *Samson et Dalila*, unknown to me, with the understanding that I might not like them as much as I did the Italians, but with the hope that I would at least give them a try.

In the summer of 1970, I left Beachwood Canyon, although my sister continued to live in the small garage apartment, and moved into Dick's rented beach house on the Pacific Coast Highway, which he shared with Roman Polanski. Dick had worked with Roman on *Rosemary's Baby* two years earlier, and had been in London with Roman when Roman's agent called with the news that Sharon had been killed. Roman and Dick had returned to Los Angeles together, Roman crying in Dick's arms during the long plane trip home. As he could not live in the house on Cielo Drive, Roman had moved into the beach house with Dick and was still living there when I arrived with my boxes of books. Although the murders had been solved, I would often find amiable homicide detectives in shirtsleeves and shoulder holsters sitting on the deck with Roman, chatting and drinking. Roman, despite the rumors, had never been a suspect, and the detectives were fond of him. Like most policemen, they were also excited by celebrity.

Roman was a talkative, nervous, impatient creature. I towered over him, but as I was invisible, it did not matter. I was too old to interest him, which allowed me to wander through the house as I pleased. I was also Dick's girlfriend, although that would not necessarily have deterred him had he fancied me. If attention were diverted from him for even an instant, he fell into a performance of manic devilment, not unlike Rumpelstiltskin, which usually was sufficient to gain him an audience. If I cooked roast lamb, I was thanked, but told that he had a much better recipe, one that required forty cloves of garlic. If he found *Anna Karenina* on a table where I'd left it, he would tell Dick to let me know that Dostoevsky was a better writer. If he saw me bodysurfing in front of the house with a boogie board, he said that in Poland, where, he claimed, bodysurfing was a national sport, he had, unlike me, never needed a fin. It was an endless competition, even with me, a hardly significant contestant, but he could not help himself. Not that it made me feel any better, but he was worse with men.

Roman Polanski, my sometime roommate, Cannes, 1976

Roman's friend and fellow Pole Jerzy Kosinski often visited from New York, and the two of them were so overwhelming that I would have to leave the house in order to breathe. Kosinski complained endlessly about America's imperial delirium, as he called it, all the while extolling the simple pleasures of Poland, which, after reading his books, I assumed he'd fled as soon as he was able to escape. He prided himself on exhibiting a pointless contrariness. I soon learned that no matter which side, which point of view was presented, although not by me, as I knew to keep my mouth shut, he would contest it with an authority that verged on hysteria, lecturing thunderously on subjects as seemingly incompatible as Heidegger and Pop-Tarts. There were many times when there was reason to believe he had his facts wrong, but no one but Roman was foolish enough to contradict him. Although he could be funny, he had no restraint, no delicacy, no modesty. Dick told me that Kosinski had been known to hide in a bedroom closet while his wife, Kiki, seduced an unsuspecting partner, jumping loudly from his hiding place to scare the wits out of their terrified victim. Money was then said to be given in return for discretion.

When Kosinski was in town, he and Roman would have dinner with us a few nights a week, sometimes with friends of ours like the Dunnes or Frank Conroy or the French actor Christian Marquand, who was said to have been the boyfriend of both Marlon Brando and Michelle Phillips. Roman and Jerzy would talk without pause, sometimes jumping onto tables and chairs better to tell a story, assuming the part of each character before abruptly climbing down from the furniture to drive into town to pull cheeks, an activity that baffled me until I realized their Polish accents had distorted the words "pull chicks."

Dick and I now and then went to New York if Dick had meetings there, and to see his three teenage boys from his first marriage, taking a taxi from the airport straight to Elaine's, where we would leave our suitcases in the kitchen and find a place to sit at one of the large round tables in the front. Although Elaine was determined that the restaurant not be a place for pickups, certain women—Anthea Sylbert, China Machado, Renata Adler, and Nora Ephron, among a few others—were allowed to sit alone at the tables along the wall without a husband or male companion. It was essentially a men's club, mostly writers and journalists, and at a time when print journalism had a certain prestige, if not glamour.

I would sit there silently, perhaps wedged between William Styron and David Halberstam's irritable Polish wife, Elzbieta, and listen to the men gossip about politics and books. I never said a word, not even when they were careless with their facts.

One would expect them to be witty and clever, and they were, but they were also very pleased with themselves. There was, not surprisingly, a lot of drinking, which, when combined with Elaine's habit of selective accounting, sometimes produced surprising results. Nelson Aldrich once burst into tears when he was given his tab at the end of a long night and saw that he had ordered twenty-seven drinks. One night, Joan Simon, who was there with her husband, Neil Simon, almost knocked over the table when she jumped to her feet, screaming, "Frank Sinatra is here! What should I do?" Now and then, arguments that had been simmering all night flared into violence, causing those writers who had never fought in their lives to resort to bites and the occasional scratch. Another night, after Kenneth Tynan spent an hour trying to convince a bored Shirley MacLaine of the exhilarating benefits of Wilhelm Reich's orgone box, she managed to escape to another table and did not return.

When we were in New York, my brother would come from Philadelphia to visit us, spending the night on a sofa in our hotel room, and Dick's three boys would come by each day after school. I would order room service for them as Dick looked on, unhappy at the expense, even though the hotel bill would be paid by the movie company or producer for whom he was then working. I had not been kind to them at first, the oldest boy only a few years younger than me. Dick complained about the child support payments he was required to make to his former wife, Carol, who had divorced him for his insistent infidelity. I loyally took his side against her, even though I knew that she was blameless. When I shoved his middle son, Jon, during an argument over who would sit in the passenger seat of Dick's Land Rover, the thought that I could be unkind to a child, conduct reminiscent of my stepmother, filled me with shame. I understood that Dick would be of no help, and one night, I went into the bathroom and wrote a letter to Carol. I told her that I wanted to be a good stepmother, and that I was not her enemy. She wrote back immediately, and while she did not give me any particular advice, our new alliance freed me of my jealousy. The boys and I became friends. I no longer set traps for them, and Jon conceded to me the front seat of the Land Rover. They even began to tell me their secrets. Suddenly, Dick was the outsider, but as it was a position he seemed to prefer, everyone was, for the moment, content.

With my youngest stepson, Mark,
Connecticut, 1970

In Los Angeles, we moved into an apartment in the somewhat derelict Chateau Marmont that had a narrow cement balcony overlooking the Strip, and a small kitchen with a stained linoleum floor. One night, a girl knocked on the door. She held a brown paper bag, which she opened cautiously to reveal a young calico cat, whose eyes were completely black. The girl said that she and the cat, a female, had taken acid earlier in the evening, but that the cat had turned vicious.

The cat now appeared to be paralyzed. She was on her way to the garbage chute to dispose of it when she remembered that she'd seen me earlier in the Chateau's underground garage and had decided that I looked like a nice person. She had asked the desk clerk who sold her the acid my name and the number of our apartment. I lifted the little cat from the garbage bag and held her motionless against my chest for the next twelve hours. After two days, she began to eat and drink. She lived with me for many years, but I never once heard her make a sound.

Mike Nichols and his wife, Annabel Davis-Goff, and
Richard Avedon, New York, 1985

In 1971, Dick began work on the film *Carnal Knowledge*, which was written by Jules Feiffer and would be directed by Mike Nichols. While Dick was looking for possible locations, I mentioned that he should see Ale Kaiser's new apartment in New York, which had been designed and, in an unusual gesture, decorated by Paul Rudolph. We went to New York to see the apartment, which was on the thirty-first and thirty-second floors of a new building at 860 UN Plaza. Two walls of the large living room were made of glass, allowing a vertiginous view of the East River and the Brooklyn shoreline. The furniture, much of it Lucite, was upholstered in white leather. Rudolph had cut hundreds of small silver balls in two and glued them to the ceiling. The carpets were white fur, perhaps polar bear. There was a mother-of-pearl table from the Forbidden Palace. The only color in the room was a Frank Stella mural that Ale had bought from Leo Castelli for seventeen thousand dollars. There was also a white standard poodle. Dick was, as I'd expected, surprised by the outlandish beauty of it, and he designed a set for *Carnal Knowledge* that was almost identical to Ale's apartment, although without the dog.

Dick had worked on Mike's previous films, including *The Graduate*, and had won an Oscar for production design for *Who's Afraid of Virginia Woolf*. They were friends, but not intimates. I sometimes found it tiring to be around Mike. Too great displays of brilliance can be trying. He led the conversation and, like Ivan Moffat, too often resorted to anecdote. Despite his funny stories, some of them heard more than once, I was nervous in his company. I felt that he, too, was never fully at ease. I was interested to see that Dick did not make any attempt to match him in wit, but was content, at least in public, to appear amused. Although I felt smarter and funnier when I was with Mike, especially if I could make him laugh, I learned to be wary of him, as others must have done, too. Years later, he became a generous and kind friend, but in those early days, his sharp wit could be wounding.

As a production designer, Dick would begin work on a

movie months before anyone else, choosing locations as well as designing sets and overseeing their construction. For tax reasons as well as the cheaper production costs, *Carnal Knowledge* would be made in Vancouver. As I was going to Canada with Dick, it seemed like a good time to quit my job. After eight months of a desultory reading of bad scripts and much shopping, I told Warren that he needed to find another script reader.

The movie company rented a house for us in a suburb of the city called Deep Cove. We drove to Vancouver in the Land Rover, a converted troop carrier complete with gas stove and refrigerator, stopping along the way to fly fish for trout and steelhead. We listened to a tape of *Abbey Road* over and over again as we slowly drove north, eating Manischewitz matzo bread and drinking Cokes. We would sleep in the Land Rover at night, the sound of a nearby river tumbling through my head, but it was cramped and difficult to sleep as we were both tall. We left the heavy back door ajar so that our feet could hang over the bumper, and in the morning, my pajamas would be wet with dew. Dick was a skillful fisherman, making his own rods and flies, and he taught me how to fish at a time when it was unusual to see a woman fly fishing in an American river. He was most himself when he found himself in a river at dusk, a fly rod in hand, casting the delicate dry fly he had just made to match the hatch, as fishermen say, into the dark and deep pool where he knew a trout lay hidden. We would wade in different parts of a river so as not to distract or impede each other, and when it grew too dark to fish and I would no longer frighten the trout, I would pull off my heavy rubber waders and slip into the cold river. I could smell the smoke from Dick's pipe as he waited for me on the bank, and hear the click of his Zippo lighter as he relit his pipe, his face now and then illuminated by the flame of the lighter.

I understood that a certain harshness of character could come from suffering, but I did not think that childhood distress tended to ennoblement, or provided any particular moral endowment. Dick's life, as far as I knew, had not been particularly difficult. I also questioned the common conceit that hardship and trouble were conducive to making an artist. Dickens is often used as an example of this in that his traumatic childhood is assumed to have induced in him a hatred of cruelty to children and a need to write about it, but surely most writers abhor cruelty to children, even if they don't choose to write about it.

Dick had a certain rigidity of character, resulting in secrecy and even a contempt of others, but as he had learned to temper his inherent dissatisfaction with wit, and as he was not unkind or condescending to me, I chose to see it as a sign of his intelligence, rather than a flaw. While he was not free with his sympathy, his thinking was liberal and sometimes even adventurous, which allowed me to overlook his occasional failure of heart. His dislike of his own Jewish descent, so strong as to lead him to assume what he naively imagined were the appearance and habits of an English gentleman and to prefer women who were not Jewish, came, he said, from an abhorrence of being forced by his family, particularly his grandmother, into an identity that did not suit him. When I suggested that the assumptions of his relatives were those of first- and second-generation European Jews who had immigrated to America, many of whom had survived the Holocaust, he said that of course I was right, but that he had no intention of becoming a member of what he called "that club." For a long time, his mother, in my presence, referred to me not by my name, but as the shiksa, which I chose to view as humorous, rather than as the insult it was intended to be.

I had begun to notice that Dick's capacity for sustaining sexual desire was as limited as his capacity for other pleasures. In the beginning of our love affair, he had been passionate, but his ardor had soon become merely affectionate, which confused me. I had already noticed that it is often the person who has been most offended or harmed who will then have to make everything all right. I suggested couples therapy, a solution that did not thrill me, but one that I thought might help, as we would at least be encouraged to share responsibility. I was learning to accept the terms and conditions attached to life, particularly those determined by relationships, but I needed his help. He refused to see a therapist and he refused to talk about it, implying that his lack of interest in sex was an acceptable and inevitable result of familiarity, and a condition which caused him no particular regret.

Many years later, when Dick was seeing an English friend of mine named Lizzie Spender, she came to tea with me in New York. I had not thought to question her, had never thought of it, but I suddenly heard myself ask, "Have you noticed with Dick—" Before I could finish, she interrupted me to say, "Can't fuck you after the first three months?" She smiled and I smiled, but I was shocked. "It had nothing to do with you," she said with a wave of her hand. "It happens with a lot of men." As she was the daughter of Stephen Spender and was to marry Barry Humphries, I felt that she had ample experience in the fluidity of male sexuality, and that I would do well to adopt her breezy lack of concern, which I tried, without much success, to do.

The house at Deep Cove overlooked the water, not far from the woods where Malcolm Lowry had written *Under the Volcano*. When we arrived, I discovered that the owners had left behind a young brown-and-white dog, part collie, whom they had tied to a rotting wooden doghouse. I immediately untied him and to my relief, he did not run away. I encouraged him to come inside, where he lived for the next five months.

My brother Rick came to stay with us. He had recently graduated from Villanova and expected that he would soon be drafted. He had thought about becoming a medic, as he knew that he would not be able to serve in combat. His anxiety had increased one night in Elaine's, where he was having dinner with me and Dick at a table filled with regulars, when Kosinski, who had just joined us, wondered aloud why my brother was not in Vietnam, adding that it was likely for the best, as given the look of him, he would be "eaten alive within an hour of landing in Saigon." As my brother was not someone who could be described as frail or delicate, or effeminate, as may have been Kosinski's intimation, I could only assume that Kosinski was, as usual, demanding attention and employing rudeness to get it. With the help of Jules Feiffer, my brother spoke to William Sloane Coffin, the civil rights activist who was chaplain at Yale and later served at Riverside Church in New York, and was a fervent opponent of the war. He suggested that my brother abandon any plan to go to Canada and instead apply for conscientious objector status as a pacifist. If his suit was successful, it was possible that the alternative service he would be obliged to perform might then require him to serve as medic. It would be necessary for Rick to collect certain papers, including reference letters, and he had come to Vancouver in part so that I could help him to organize and complete his application. The board before whom he would appear would consist of our grandmother's neighbors, many of whom had served in the Second World War, men who might not look favorably on a college graduate with long hair and a beard who was hoping to avoid the draft. His particular judges would be the local butcher from whom I used to collect my aunt's roasts, and the greengrocer, and the pharmacist, hardworking men, second-generation Italians and Poles and Irishmen, all of them Catholic, all of them proud to be citizens of the United States.

I knew almost no men or women who were in Vietnam. My first boyfriend, Billy Quinn, was a pilot in the air force. He had suffered some hostility from childhood companions, including me, when it was discovered that he had enlisted. My mother's younger brother, known as Bad Uncle Joe, was in Saigon with the marines, working on an LST. He was inclined to trouble, some of which occasionally required his presence in the brig, and there was a family rumor that he was the father of a half-Vietnamese child, but he was not given to letter writing and I knew little, if anything, about his time there.

When I lived in Beverly Hills, I had not gone to marches or demonstrations, either in protest of the war or the assassination of Martin Luther King or the violence in Chicago. I signed petitions and wrote letters, but other than my work in Watts, which I was aware was to my emotional benefit as well as that of the children, I was content to help in my own small way, which I understood was partly a form of penance for my mother's death. Many years later, I taught English to a group of young men who had been in juvenile detention or had recently been released from Rikers Island in Manhattan in the hope that they would earn a high school equivalency, which was in some cases a condition of their parole. In the memoirs that I asked them to write, I read that many of them had grandfathers and uncles and cousins who were Vietnam veterans. When I asked them to tell me more about these men, I realized that they had no idea of Vietnam, either as a place or a war. I asked if they'd like to know more, and they were interested, especially as many of their relatives had had a hard time of it, trouble which was understood to have been caused by the war itself. I decided to show them the film *Hearts and Minds*, the documentary made by Peter Davis, rather than attempt to teach a necessarily superficial history of the war which would have bored and confused them. A few minutes into the film, I began to wonder if I had made a mistake. Without needing or wishing to have more information, more history, they were instantly on the side of the Vietnamese, outraged and horrified by the footage of American F-4 Phantoms bombing old men, women, and children. Some of the boys began to pace back and forth across the dark classroom, now and then shouting loudly at the screen. I had to stop the film several times to answer their questions and to allow them to calm themselves. The alienation, drug addiction, and mental illnesses of those relatives who had served in Vietnam suddenly began to make sense to them, and they saw that the damaged men had been as much victimized by the policies of the United States as were the Vietnamese. We somehow got through the film, having to watch it over two days, given their frequent eruptions of fury. The hatred and mistrust of government that they already felt was intensified, as was their wish for revenge on behalf of the Vietnamese people and those relatives of their own who had suffered, as well as for those who had died in Vietnam. Although I was chastised by my mentor at the school for agitating the already emotionally fragile students, both he and I, in the end, did not think that it had been a mistake to show them Peter's film.

My brother left Deep Cove to return to Philadelphia, where he succeeded, to everyone's surprise and relief, in gaining the status of conscientious objector. He began his alternative two-year service, somewhat inexplicably, not as a medic but as head of the film program at the campus ministry center of the University of Pennsylvania, where he sensibly showed only those movies that interested him, most of them foreign films.

Once my brother left, the abandoned dog and I and the silent calico cat spent the day in solitude. It was too cold to swim in the cove, but we went for walks, and I read, of course. As the days were long, I asked Dick if there was any work that I could do on the movie. I could help him select wallpaper for a set, or find just the right ashtray or teapot needed for a scene. While he said that he could not give me work, most of which was unionized, he suggested that I accompany him to the studio. I was hesitant to do this, as I was afraid that I would be a distraction, if not a burden, and I did not accept his invitation.

In the first week of rehearsals, Mike received a call from Otto Preminger, who was making a movie of the novel *Such Good Friends* in New York. Otto was casting the female lead, and John and Joan had, to my astonishment, told Preminger that he should consider me for the part. Rather than fly me to New York for a reading, not that I had agreed to such an unlikely undertaking, Preminger asked Mike if he would shoot a few minutes of film of me. I could not imagine what had made the Dunnes do such a thing. I tried to wiggle out of it, but both

Dick and Mike, who I suspect found it momentarily diverting, encouraged me to do it. An actor named Cynthia O'Neal, who had a small part in Mike's movie, read lines with me, and the scene was filmed with great seriousness by Mike's cinematographer, Giuseppe Rotunno, who was Fellini's cameraman. As it quickly became evident that I was not very good, Mike asked me to work on some needlepoint that I happened to have with me, in order to keep my hands busy, a detail Joan later used in one of her novels. The footage was sent to Otto, who, to no one's surprise, cast Jennifer O'Neill in the role.

My screen test with Mike Nichols, on the set of
*Carnal Knowledge*, Vancouver, 1971

I could feel that I was slipping into the melancholia that always lay in wait for me, and I asked Dick if I could change my mind and now and then visit him on the set. When I promised to stay out of his way, he shook his head and smiled. "You are never in my way," he said. The actors in the movie were Candice Bergen, Ann-Margret, Art Garfunkel, and Jack Nicholson. I knew Candy, but I did not know the others. I soon found myself next to Jack or Art, perhaps at the communal lunch table or waiting on the set. Their rented house had a swimming pool, and Art, with whom I talked about books, encouraged me to use it while they were working, and on the days that I did not go to the set, I went there to swim. One afternoon when I arrived, both of them were in the pool. When Jack hoisted himself onto the side of the hot tub, I saw that he was naked. Art was naked, too. They were completely at ease, but I was embarrassed, especially as I realized that I was expected to be naked, too. They could see that I was uncomfortable and it amused them, which made me feel even more like a prude. I wasn't a prude, but I was still shy about things like nudity, not that I wanted anyone to know it, especially not Jack Nicholson and Art Garfunkel. Jack toppled into the pool and swam to the shallow end where I was standing, my legs in the water. He was having fun, and showing off for Art when he stood next to me. Rather than look away, I forced myself to look at his penis, as small and as pink as a nestling, causing him to lower himself into the water. Slowly, his mouth open, his beautiful teeth bared in a wide grin, he sank beneath the surface.

As perhaps was inevitable, given his boredom and my loneliness, I began to visit Jack each day in his dressing room. I tried to look my prettiest, abandoning the bell-bottomed jeans and Converse sneakers that had replaced Mrs. Kaiser's dresses and shoes to wear the cotton cheongsams and embroidered black satin slippers I'd found in Chinatown in downtown Vancouver. He was still a working-class boy from Neptune, New

Jersey, with an instinctive Irish gallantry, as well as a cheerful, lackadaisical tolerance of almost everything, a trait that I found irritating in others, but which I found instructive in Jack, especially after the sometimes chilly intellectualism of Mike and Dick. His ideas were not thought out fully, and because he talked fast, he sometimes didn't make sense. He wandered here and there when he spoke, which made it hard to follow him. Unlike me, there were no airs about him. While I was selective to the point of strain, he was so encompassing that he sometimes strayed into banality. He had been reading about Napoleon and he told me that when Napoleon was in exile on Elba, one of his servants made him a tiny chariot to which he had tied six mice. "When the mice were too scared to move, Napoleon twisted their tails together and they took off, dragging the carriage behind them. What a genius." He would tell me stories like this, and then smile at me madly. Although he had about him a certain innocence, his manic grin reminded me of the wolf who ate Red Riding Hood, a not unappealing association.

He liked to hear about my childhood in the Islands, and I would tell him some of the stories I had once told my grandmother, careful to remove anything that suggested triumph over adversity, a theme which I abhorred when applied to myself. The only time that I ever disagreed with him was when he said that I had to admire Hitler for his determination, as Hitler had held to his beliefs. I was furious. I still believed that there could be no excellence without virtue, a view that I realized might be seen, at least by Jack, as anachronistic and even a bit romantic. I believed that most people knew the difference between right and wrong, and if they found they had made the wrong choice, they had no one to blame but themselves. I had recently read an essay by Hannah Arendt in which she wrote that evil would be the great problem of postwar intellectual life, as death had been the fundamental problem after the First World War, but I was afraid to argue with him, fearful that it would cause me to think less of him. Of course, it is possible that he felt the same about me. As gentle and as malleable as he then was with women, he had a certain fondness for tyrants.

We both understood what it meant to be on location, with all of its implicit pleasures and inevitable abandonments, but we were also somewhat nervously aware that we were on the verge of something. Although the door to his dressing room was kept closed, there were constant interruptions. Makeup needed him for a touch-up, or the script girl had pages that Jules had just added to the script, or Art, knowing that I would be with Jack, came to chat with me about Turgenev. Art was a very good reader, which surprised me, as I had not known that pop stars were in the habit of reading nineteenth-century Russian novels. The interruptions, as frequent as they were, were not consequential, as there was nothing untoward about my time with Jack. We were both so aware of each other, so tense with excitement, that we were careful not to touch each other as we passed through a doorway, and soon made a point of sitting at different ends of the lunch table. Anyone paying attention must have seen what was happening, but Dick seemed not to notice my euphoria. As Jack and I had not even kissed each other, we were spared the squalor of deceit, not out of probity, but because there was no place for us to meet in private. There is a slide show in the film, assembled by Jack's character, of all the girls in his life, with cynical even contemptuous remarks about each of them. He asked me if I would give him a photograph of myself to include in the slide show, and I did, flattered to be included in what was called "Ballbusters on Parade."

As Jack's work on the film was soon to be completed, he worried that once we returned to Los Angeles, he would not be able to see me. He wondered if I would consider working for him as a script reader. I, of course, agreed without hesitation.

I found a home for the dog, and Dick and I returned to Los Angeles, where we moved into an apartment building on La Cienega, just south of Sunset, which had been designed to resemble a Japanese manor house. It was unlike anything else in town, and it was appropriately called The Lotus. Early on, I had arranged it so that there were certain domestic chores that I would gladly do, and other things that I would not do (iron). I would make food. I would not toss laundry onto the floor. I would not leave dirty dishes in the sink, not that I wanted to leave dishes in the sink. Freud believed that women were made the guardians of fire because they could not yield to the impulse, common to men, to urinate on fire and extinguish it. That was me. I was not urinating on anything.

In order to have an excuse to see each other, Jack suggested that we meet at his house at the top of Mulholland Drive to discuss the scripts and manuscripts that I read each week. I no longer had a car, having given my silver Opel to my sister, and Jack would pick me up in his Volkswagen. There were always a number of people at his house, usually men, some of them friends from high school, who wandered in and out of the house to sit in the hot tub or to make big pots of spaghetti Bolognese or to shoot BB guns at the neighbors' cats. There was a voluble, wild-eyed Greek woman named Helena, who attempted to manage the house, as well as a housekeeper who did the cooking and cleaning. A tall bearded man named Red Dog made sure that there were ample supplies of drugs. An amused young woman named Ann Marshall was Jack's secretary. Her father was the English actor Herbert Marshall. Jack had never seen Marshall in a film, and I explained that he had exemplified a certain continental worldliness, an attribute that was no longer considered necessary in a movie star. "Like me, you mean?" he asked, and then laughed.

To move from the dark living room to his bedroom required several visits, but we at last climbed the carpeted stairs to his room, where he locked the door and put a cassette of the Ink Spots into a boom box on his bedside table. The knowledge that people were wandering about the house, perhaps even listening to us, made me so uncomfortable that I jumped at the slightest sound, causing him to ask if anything was wrong, a question that further unnerved me. As I did not like my face to be seen during intercourse, I asked him to close the curtains, which turned out to be harder than I'd imagined, as the cords were tangled. I needed to be in darkness because I feared that my expression would give away all that I felt, good and bad, and would in consequence allow my partner to know too much about me. Somehow, if my eyes were closed and I was invisible in the dark, I could hold on to what little power I felt I possessed.

Our time in bed did not go badly, but it was not thrilling. The longing that had so exhilarated us in Vancouver did not make it to the upstairs bedroom on Mulholland Drive. The first time that we made love, he politely asked if I wanted to leave Dick. I could always stay with him, he said. He seemed relieved when I did not answer him. Later, he sat naked on the edge of the bed and slapped both of his thighs before turning to me to say, "If these were five inches longer, I'd have been a star five years sooner."

When we no longer troubled to climb the stairs to his room, I wondered if Dick was right, after all, when he said that boredom was the inevitable result, even a condition of passion. This was to remain a mystery to me for some time. One afternoon when Jack dropped me off later than usual, I found that Dick was already at home. At the sight of him, I was so overwhelmed with guilt that I rushed to the bathroom and vomited into the toilet. He came after me in concern and asked, "Is everything okay with you?" "Not really," I said, and we left it at that.

With Dick during the filming of
*The Day of the Dolphin*, Abaco, 1972

Jack soon fell in love with Michelle Phillips, and his reports of her merciless torments helped to advance my limited understanding of sexual enticement. He told me that she would only allow him to touch certain parts of her body when they made love. "Sometimes it's her back, and then it's her ass," he said, "but not her face or her tits." The rules changed depending on her mood. When I said that I was sorry, he looked at me in disappointment. "But I love it," he said. He owned a small house next to his own, and Michelle had moved into it with her little girl and her Mexican housekeeper. Jack would wake in the morning to discover the distinctive racing car of the man with whom she was also having an affair parked in his driveway. He would then call me to ask if I would make him some stuffed cabbage, one of his favorite things to eat, which he would devour in my kitchen, standing at the counter while he talked about Michelle. I, who had considered myself shamefully amoral given my own infidelity, was clearly an amateur. Years later, when he was living with Anjelica Huston, who did not know that I'd had a romance with Jack before she knew him, not that she would have minded, she told me that he was the best lover she'd ever had, and it occurred to me that perhaps it was I who had been disappointing, not Jack.

TEN

That summer, I met Josie Mankiewicz Davis, always introduced as the daughter of the man who'd written *Citizen Kane*,
a work of genius for which he had not been given sufficient
credit by Orson Welles. She was married to Peter Davis, who
was making the documentary about Vietnam that years later I
showed my students from Rikers Island, and she became my
first intimate female friend since adolescence. Plump, not too
tall, sometimes a little stoned, which I did not at first realize as
I thought that she was simply amused by my insistent need to
make sense of things, which caused her to laugh at me almost
without pause. She was very attuned to the absurdities of popular culture and she could name, if asked, all of the celebrities
who had been born or died on that particular day. She insisted,

sometimes to the despair of her husband, on using only packaged or bottled or canned ingredients when cooking, as in her recipe for chicken Arlene Francis, which called for a chicken and apricot jam. Her cookies, which required no baking, were made with corn syrup, Jif peanut butter, and Kellogg's cornflakes. This reflected her dislike of domestic chores, as well as her somewhat anarchic humor, but it led me to cook with only the most natural, hardest to find, freshest ingredients, which, among other exacting tasks, meant tracking down a butcher whose meat had never been frozen. Arugula was not yet known in America, and Camilla McGrath brought me seeds from Italy, which I grew in large pots. I used a French cookbook, *Simca's Cuisine*, which I went through recipe by recipe, as well as the cookbooks of Mildred Knopf, given to me years earlier by Connie, and Diana Kennedy's book of Mexican food. I made my own sourdough bread, yoghurt, smoked fish, pasta, tortillas, chocolate truffles, pâté, and chutneys. Even at the time, it seemed excessive, if not desperate. Josie's quick recipes contained a hint of mockery, while mine, as difficult to make as possible, were grandiose.

Josie liked for us to lie on her bed in the afternoon before her two boys came home from school, where we would try to fall asleep in an attempt to capture that moment between consciousness and mindlessness when disparate, nonsensical thoughts flit through the mind. Those strange visitations came to her easily, perhaps because of the marijuana that she liked to smoke, and she would describe her fleeting visions, so distracting me that it was impossible to have a vision of my own. Despite my failure at her game of induced dreams, we had, in our different ways, been paying attention to the same things all of our lives. Her eccentricity made me feel that I was not as unstable as I sometimes feared. I was a little in love with her.

I began to give dinner parties at the La Cienega apartment, cooked by me in our little kitchen with growing ease and confidence. One night, shortly after the release of the movie *Don't Look Now*, I asked the director of the film, Nick Roeg, to dinner. I invited Warren, too, unaware that he believed the false rumor that Nick had made for his own use and that of a few friends a short film using outtakes of a scene between Julie Christie and Donald Sutherland in *Don't Look Now*, in which it was said they had made love. When Nick arrived, Warren asked him to go outside with him. We watched through the window in astonishment as he punched Nick in the face. He then pulled Nick to his feet, examined his upper lip, and led him back into the apartment.

During those periods between movies, sometimes lasting for months, when Dick did not work, he would paint and I, as always, would read. He wrote a screenplay of *Jacob's Room* in the hope of directing it himself. To his disappointment, no one was interested, finding the story incomprehensible in its subtlety. When I lived with Robby, we had often been invited to screenings of new films, and Connie had been able to order any film she wanted, provided it had been made by Fox, but I had seen very few foreign movies. Once when my father and stepmother were away for the weekend, the husband of our housekeeper at Portlock, a Frenchman named Emil, took a neighbor and me to see *Sundays and Cybèle*, a movie about a French pilot who accidentally kills a child in Vietnam and subsequently suffers from amnesia. My friend and I sobbed the whole way home in Emil's car, and he did not ask us again.

I read in the paper that there was a three-week festival of films by Kurosawa, Mizoguchi, and Ozu at an art house in Los Feliz, followed by a series of classic French films. We went to the movies every night for several months. We saw one of Dick's favorite movies, *Les Enfants du Paradis,* as well as films by Renoir, Chabrol, Vigo, and Jean-Pierre Melville. Naturally, I wondered what had taken me so long.

John and Joan moved from Franklin Avenue to a house on a bluff overlooking the Pacific Ocean at Trancas. My sister Tina began to work for them as Joan's private secretary and as a companion to Quintana, collecting her at school each afternoon and helping her with her homework. Tina called me one day to say that she had discovered that Joan used engraved stationery. She was upset by this, as her idea of an artist did not encompass the use of expensive letter paper. I told her that it did not in any way betray Joan's finer self, and that it was not a sign of bourgeois decadence, as she feared, but she would hear none of it, and always viewed it as one of Joan's few faults. I did not tell her, then or ever, that Joan had occasionally published articles in the *National Review,* lest, given her standards, she quit her job.

Harrison Ford, who was beginning to find small parts in movies, was hired by the Dunnes to build bookcases and a redwood deck in the new house. He and my sister fell in love, and although he was married, they began to see each other at her apartment in West Hollywood, where he preferred to climb through a bathroom window rather than use the front door. Thirty years later, he asked me to apologize to her for his treatment of her. It was not something that I felt I could say to her and I suggested that he tell her himself, which I knew he would not do.

Dick began work on a new film, *Fat City*, and we drove north to the San Joaquin Valley in the Land Rover, again stopping along the way to fish for trout and steelhead. The actors in the movie were Stacy Keach, Jeff Bridges, Candy Clark, and Susan Tyrrell. Leonard Gardner, who had written the adaptation of his own novel, was also in Stockton, a farm town that Dick had chosen as the film's location. The director, John Huston, and the cinematographer, Conrad Hall, stayed in rented houses on a bluff overlooking the San Joaquin River, but we lived with the cast and crew in a motel with a small swimming pool. It was very hot and some days there would be thirty people in the pool. As Dick was busy selecting places to shoot and building sets, Leonard and I spent each afternoon in a dark Mexican bar in downtown Stockton, drinking Dos Equis and talking about books.

On the weekends, Dick, Leonard, and I went to the boxing matches held in the civic arena. *Fat City* is a story about Latino bantamweights, among other things, and Leonard knew many of the boxers, delicate and pale boys, their broken noses and scarred brows the only indications that they were fighters. The arena would be full of migrant workers, as well as ranch hands and farmers from the Valley. The fights were rough and raucous, and there were frequent brawls among the spectators. Some of the men at the matches carried fighting cocks in handmade wire cages.

A former Santa Anita jockey named Billy Pearson, who had for years smuggled on Huston's behalf pre-Columbian artifacts and other treasures from Mexico and Central America into the country, was also there, and I so disapproved of him that I would not go to the fights if Pearson was going, too. Susan Tyrrell would often come with us, wandering off with a few of the fighters, not always the victors, at the end of the night. She visited Huston above the river each afternoon to give him a blow job. "It's not as bad as you'd think," she said, "except for his fucking oxygen tank, which bangs against my head. Here, feel the lumps." There were other complaints about Huston, as he was old and tired. Although he appeared each day on the set, accompanied by Pearson and his elderly secretary, Gladys, it was Dick and Conrad Hall who directed the movie, making the necessary decisions as to lighting and editing, and even the performances. Leonard and I wrote to each other after he returned to San Francisco and we went home to Los Angeles, but as happens, we eventually stopped writing, a lapse that filled me with regret.

MIKE NICHOLS, preparing to direct *The Day of the Dolphin*, a story based on research done by John Lilly, a neuroscientist who claimed that he could teach dolphins to speak English, asked Dick to design the film. Dick did not think that the script, written by Buck Henry from a book by Robert Merle, was any good, but he agreed to work on the film. We spent a month flying in small planes to coastal villages in Mexico, as well as to various islands in the Caribbean, while he looked for locations, spending a few extra days at each place to fly fish for mahi mahi, permit, and bonefish. Saltwater fly fishing had yet to become popular, and the crews on the boats that Dick chartered had never seen a fly rod. To Dick's fury, many fish were lost when a deckhand mistakenly grabbed the delicate tippet to pull a hooked fish into the boat. I disliked fishing for mahi mahi. As they travel in pairs, chum would first be thrown into the water to attract a fish, which was then caught on a conventional saltwater lure and held in the water close to the boat. Its mate would swim to it in distress, at which point Dick would cast to it. When both fish were pulled into the boat, their luminous, translucent color, blue and purple and green, would drain from their bodies within seconds, leaving them gray and lifeless.

Dick at last decided on the island of Abaco in the Bahamas, where a new resort called Treasure Cay had recently been built. He began construction of an extensive compound of docks, dolphin pens, and marine biology laboratories. Many of the houses at Treasure Cay had not yet been bought and the movie company rented a dozen of them for the actors and crew. There was little fresh food on the island, other than limes, conch, and barracuda. Once a week, when the barge from Nassau was in port, I made the long drive on a dusty white coral road to the main town of Marsh Harbor to buy food. The island itself was flat, with impenetrable swamps of mangrove, and an interior dense with palms and white pine. At low tide, the flats had a sour, rotten smell, but there was a white sand beach in front of the hotel at Treasure Cay with hundreds of rare shells, so many shells that I soon began to kick the lesser specimens aside as I walked through the shallows, feeling for yet another chambered nautilus with my toes. I swam each day, and I read, as Dick had arranged for the movie company to ship dozens of boxes of books to the location. It was on Abaco that I first read Proust.

Jack at the airport, Abaco, 1972

Dick found a local Bahamian fisherman named Hartman Russell to pole us across the flats each late afternoon in a Boston whaler that Dick had appropriated from the movie, and which he later gave in payment to Hartman. We fished for permit, snook, and bonefish, which are difficult to catch. If Hartman, who worked as a carpenter, could not take us in the boat, we would walk across the clay flats, looking for the upended tails of bonefish as they burrowed for food. Sometimes I would be surrounded by dozens of small sharks, which I chased away by slapping the water with the tip of my rod. There was the maddening torment of no-see-ums, which flew into my eyes and nose and ears by the thousands, causing me to run to shore and the refuge of the car.

Although I had been disheartened by the landscape when we first arrived, I soon came to see the beauty of it. I knew from my reading, and in particular from Proust, that for some, the fantasy of travel, the expectation of new provocations is preferable to the disappointment that inevitably awaits one upon arrival, but I did not feel that way. I always expected to be pleased and I was never disappointed. The flats were lavender in the light of the setting sun, their surface broken at low tide by the bubbling air holes of crabs and sea cucumbers. Blue herons stalked through the mangrove, silent and alert. At night when I could not sleep, I stood at the salt-encrusted sliding glass doors of the bungalow to watch enormous land crabs emerge disjointedly from their tunnels in the sand, two feet tall, their bulbous eyes on stalks half a foot long, an invading force of cannibals, clicking and clacking as they scuttled from one palm tree to the next. The first night that I saw them, I thought that I was dreaming.

In the beginning, before the rest of the crew and the big shots arrived, Dick and I spent time with the team of men who always worked with him. I was very fond of Bill Parks, who was the construction manager. During the Second World War, he had been stationed in the Pacific, moving every few days from one atoll to the next to build coral runways, only a day or two ahead of the bombers and fighter planes, and he still suffered from shell shock. He was shy and polite, addressing me as "ma'am" and lifting his baseball cap whenever he saw me, but once a month he would slip into a mild hysteria, building tree forts and doghouses, among other less functional structures. During these episodes, he was compelled to tell dirty jokes, some of which I did not understand and which Dick would have to explain to me. I remember one in particular, as I'd been embarrassed not to get it. I bumped into him as he was headed into town, where he was meeting a woman he'd met at a VFW barbecue in Marsh Harbor, and he asked me if he looked all right. "Very handsome," I said. "Well," he said, grinning in anticipation, "if you can't cut the mustard, you can always lick the jar." I had no idea what he was talking about and later told Dick that sadly Bill's most recent mania had him talking about condiments.

Mike Nichols and Annabel Davis-Goff, the woman with whom he lived, soon arrived on Abaco, along with Buck Henry and Brooke Hayward, and the actors George C. Scott, his wife Trish Van Devere, and Paul Sorvino. Roberto, Mike's chef from Connecticut, would prepare lunch each day for the crew, somewhat unsuccessfully as it turned out, as his recipes were too refined. There were bitter denunciations of his delicious rice pudding made with rose water and cardamom, said by the crew to resemble semen. The script supervisor on the film was a handsome older woman named Meta Carpenter Wilde. She was one of Mike's favorites and had also worked on *Who's Afraid of Virginia Woolf?* and *The Graduate*. Dick told me that she had been Faulkner's girlfriend for twenty years, having met him in Hollywood in the Thirties. Of course, I wanted to know her and to talk about Faulkner, but such a thing was not possible. Whenever I was on the set or at the communal lunch, I

Buck Henry and Mike Nichols, on the set of
*Catch-22*, Rome, 1967

could not help but stare at her. She smiled at me once or twice
when she saw me looking at her, but we never spoke. I was too
shy and she was too reserved, and perhaps wary of anyone who
might want to ask her about her past.

I tried very hard to make Annabel my friend, partly out of
loneliness, but also because I could see that she was intelligent,
but she wasn't interested in me. She was kept busy looking after
Mike, who was demanding about food, and she made complicated recipes taken from *The New York Times* while tending to
their frequent guests. When I wondered how she could possibly
find the necessary ingredients on Abaco, Dick explained that
special orders like crème fraîche and veal were sometimes included in the shipments of supplies flown to the island. I once
heard her say that Americans had a reverence for Churchill
that was undeserved. There were many abandoned dogs on
the island, some of whom I fed and washed. She disapproved

Baja, 1973

of this, believing that dogs should not be made foolish by too much affection. Is it any wonder that she fascinated me? I did not see her as much as I would have liked. One of their visitors was Lillian Hellman, who, the only afternoon that I spent in her company, corrected my pronunciation of certain words—"roman à clef," among others—for which I was grateful. I was showing off when I used the word "kempt," which I had once heard my English teacher say, and Lillian exploded with harsh laughter, shrieking, "You are looking very KEMPT today!" and

I was not grateful. Frank Conroy and my brother Rick came to stay with us, giving me an excuse to make a key lime pie every few days, using graham crackers, always a bit stale, which made for a better crust, limes that Hartman sold me, condensed milk, thick and sweet, and dozens of cans of Reddiwip.

A number of young, good-looking men and women soon appeared in Treasure Cay in neon-colored wetsuits, along with eight trained dolphins shipped from the Virgin Islands and Florida. Some of the trainers had worked for Dr. Lilly, and at Marine World and Disneyland. I never saw one of them in a bad mood, and I avoided them. One day, I was invited to swim in a tank with one of the male dolphins. I found it extremely unpleasant, even alarming. The skin of the dolphin was as rough as industrial sandpaper, unlike what I had expected from its sleek and shiny appearance. The dolphin itself was instantly aggressive, slamming into me and pushing me repeatedly and with force against the sides of the tank. I couldn't wait to get out of the water. Years later, I saw a man who had been an associate producer of the film. "Did you know I married one of the dolphin trainers?" he asked. "A gorgeous blonde, you probably don't remember her, as they were all blond and you didn't hang around that much, but she claims she was the only one who'd never had sex with a dolphin."

—————— ELEVEN ——————

$\mathbf{I}$ had taken a leave of absence, a grandiose term given my actual job, from reading scripts for Jack while I was in the Bahamas, but I resumed my work for him as soon as we returned to Los Angeles, although I no longer went to his house to pick up and deliver the scripts. As someone from time to time would mention one of my reports to me or to Dick, a friend of Jack's perhaps, but also a producer or filmmaker, I realized that the reports were being read by people other than Jack. I thought that this was not a good idea, as I often wrote criticism that was a bit harsh, primarily to keep Jack's attention and to make him laugh. I asked his agent, Sandy Bresler, if he allowed anyone other than Jack to read my reports. Well, yes, he said, he did sometimes share them with others. People thought they were funny, although some people had been offended. I asked if in the future he would keep the reports private, as they were intended to be, and he said that he would, but he didn't, causing several people around town to stop speaking to me. I was surprised by the assumption that I had the power to determine what work Jack might choose to do, when, at most, I was only doing his homework.

For some time, it had seemed to me that people decide to marry or to have a child or to buy a house at the moment that their relationship is coming to an end, in part as an attempt to save it, and because they do not know what else to do. I was no exception, and when I asked Dick to marry me, it must have seemed to him, too, like something we should do. We were married the next month in Santa Monica, with my sister Tina and Mike Nichols as witnesses. Dick gave me a wristwatch from Tiffany as a wedding present, and a reception was held for us by Paul and Anthea at their house in Beverly Hills. Connie Wald was there, and Jack and Michelle, and Mike, and the Dunnes, who suggested that we use the photographer Tim Page to take our wedding pictures. Tim had been a war photographer in Vietnam with his friend Sean Flynn, who had disappeared during the war, and Page had yet to recover from his time there, as well as a bad drug habit. The hundreds of black-and-white photographs that he later sent me were blurred and indistinct, which seemed uncomfortably apt.

Ale Kaiser asked me what I would like for a wedding present. She said that she could give me either a silver George III tea and coffee service from James Robinson in New York or three weeks on her yacht, the *Ale Kai*, which was moored in

Photograph by the Vietnam War photographer Tim Page of Jack
and Dick at my wedding party, Beverly Hills, 1972

Greece. I was interested that she would consider this a choice
I would have to consider seriously. I told her that we would like
to go to Greece, and she made arrangements for us to meet the
boat at its slip in Piraeus. I asked Dick if we might stop in other
cities on our way to Athens, and he agreed, knowing how elated
I was to go abroad. I studied Italian and Greek dictionaries,
made reading lists—Aeschylus, Euripides, and Sophocles, Sap-
pho and Cavafy—cooked only Greek dishes, read *I Promessi
Sposi*. I went a bit crazy.

We stayed in Paris at the Hotel Raphael, where the staff
knew Dick from previous visits and seemed surprised, if not
disappointed, to learn that he was married, which gave me
a moment's pause. We spent a week in Rome with Polanski,

who was living that year in a rented villa on the Appia Antica, then went to Bergamo to see the basilica, Milan to drink tea with Valentina Cortese, one of Dick's old girlfriends, Orvieto to see the black-and-white cathedral, Padua to see the Giotto frescoes, and at last Venice. I was overwrought with happiness.

We boarded Ale's boat in Piraeus. The crew was wary at first, but after a few days, they began to take an interest in the details of our journey. The cook and I fished for barbounia in the afternoon when it was too hot to sleep, the two of us in the dinghy, our knees touching as he smoked one cigarette after another and I struggled to have a conversation with him in Greek. We would sail through the night to our next port, drinking retsina with the captain as we studied maps and he described the glories that awaited us. After two days at Delos, we sailed to Kilàda, on the eastern coast of the Peloponnese, where Dick rented a rickety car from the town's mayor and we drove through the mountains to Corinth and Olympia.

From the moment that I arrived in Europe, I felt that I had finally reached the place where I was meant to be. Although I knew that my life was not in Padua or Asolo or Paris, could not be there, at least not yet, I realized that I had never felt that I was American, in part because of my fiercely Irish grandmother, and because I'd lived in Hawai'i when it was still only a territory of the United States. Rather than unsettling me, this realization left me feeling less adrift and alone.

After we returned to Los Angeles, I wrote to thank Ale and then wrote again when I did not hear from her. As this

On my honeymoon with Dick, Hydra, 1972

was unlike her, I wondered if something was wrong. I asked Michael Kaiser if I had offended her in some way. He hesitated and then said, Well, yes. It seemed that Dick had not tipped the crew, and the boat's captain had told Ale. They had been very attentive to us, even indulgent, and not, I didn't think, because they were in hope of a tip. At the same time, tips were important to them, even necessary, especially as the boat was not in constant use. The captain had shared my curiosity about ancient sites and their ruins, and had been proud that I took such an interest in his country. As well as feeling sick to my stomach at the injury that had been caused, my almost delirious experience of Greece was suddenly tainted with embarrassment. I wrote to Ale immediately, finding it difficult to explain what had happened without causing Dick to appear rude and cheap. In the end, I wrote that it was my fault. I did not know that he hadn't tipped them, but I should have made sure that he did. During the time that it took her to forgive me, I thought how striking, how ironic it would be if our long and deep attachment were brought to an end because of yet another of her many gifts and my husband's refusal to honor it.

My brother Rick moved to Los Angeles that year, and rented a little house in Venice for one hundred dollars a month. As he did not have a job, Dick suggested that he might, at least for a little while, find work at the studio as a carpenter. That his only experience of working with tools had been the construction of a fort in the scrub behind our house at Portlock did not seem to matter. Rick said that he was willing to try, and Dick took him to the Sears in Santa Monica to buy him the tools that he would need, as well as a shiny red toolbox. This turned out to be a mistake, as the newness of the tools immediately revealed that he knew nothing about carpentry. His fellow workers would have been rough on him anyway, as they were unionized and he had been given the job at Dick's direction, but the red toolbox did not help matters. Dick heard from his set dresser that Rick had been given the nickname "Crash," but Rick never said a word about it. Years later, when he had been given a union card and was a crew supervisor, I asked him about those first weeks on the job. He smiled and changed the subject.

My brother Michael had joined a commune and was living in an ashram in Honolulu, and my sister Anne had run away from home to live at a riding stable on Lunalilo Home Road, where she taught herself to ride and to care for horses. I rarely heard from them, which I thought was more my fault than their responsibility. I was not even sure that they knew where I lived.

In 1973, Dick began work on *Chinatown*, directed by Roman and written by Bob Towne. Jack was in the movie, and Faye Dunaway and John Huston. Anthea Sylbert was the costume designer, and the producer was Dick's friend Bob Evans. Bob warned Dick that if he stared at me it was only because I reminded him of his former wife, Ali MacGraw, who had broken his heart, which amused Dick, but embarrassed me. I did not go to the set often, as I wanted to watch the Watergate hearings on television. I watched all three hundred hours, alone in the house, anxious and appalled. I sometimes wondered if I was making up for the time that my father's sister had not allowed me to watch President Kennedy's funeral. I liked to think that I had a forgiving nature, but perhaps it wasn't so.

Now and then I would visit the location to sit with Jack in his trailer, although without the longing that had once tormented us both, and which I had begun to worry I would never feel again. He talked to me about girls, and his ceaseless problems with them. He was seeing Anjelica Huston, whose aloof sophistication both unnerved and excited him. When he complained that they were never alone, I suggested that he might think about limiting the number of people who daily wandered through his house, but he did not want to do that. He reminded me of Dean Martin, who had also wanted his male friends around as a way to isolate himself and to prove that he was the kind of man who had not left his real friends behind once he came to Hollywood. It also was nice to have people around who attended you without question.

That same year, Dick began work on the film *Shampoo*, which had been written by Bob Towne for Warren, and would be directed by Hal Ashby. Warren's character was inspired by the hairdresser Jay Sebring, who had been killed by Charles Manson at the house on Cielo Drive, and by Jon Peters. Both men had delighted in fooling a surprising number of gullible Beverly Hills husbands who had assumed that they were homosexual. Hal Ashby had a puckish charm, angelic really, an amiability so constant and imperturbable that I at first attributed it to marijuana. He refused to be upset by Warren's quixotic demands, as well as his tiresome need to examine every contingency, every detail, whether it was the nutritional value of his daily lunch of cottage cheese and strawberries or the chance of rain that evening. Warren thought it would be amusing to cast me in a small part, a walk-on in which I have a few lines, as he thought my high, girlish voice was incompatible with my physical self. I was embarrassed by my voice and I was hesitant to do it, but he and Dick promised that I would not be made to sound ridiculous, and they kept their word. In the movie, I say my lines as Warren tends to Lee Grant, complaining that he has made me wait (You're jealous, Hal whispered to me before the scene, causing me to cease breathing), before I walk stiffly across Dick's set to have my hair washed.

IN FEBRUARY, Patty Hearst was kidnapped, which seemed to mark the real end of the Sixties, not the murders on Cielo Drive as Joan once pronounced. One afternoon, there appeared on live television scenes of a black neighborhood in South Central Los Angeles where a house was on fire. The people inside, who refused to come out, were thought to be those members of the Symbionese Liberation Army who had kidnapped Hearst. It was also possible, reported the excited newscasters, that Patty herself was inside the house. There was the loud flap of circling helicopters, and the sirens of ambulances and fire engines. Hundreds of people gathered excitedly on the street to watch the shootout and the fire, waving away the bits of ash and occasional sparks that flew around them. It was the first time that I and everyone else watching that day saw live coverage of a house containing human beings burn to the ground. I thought of the black-and-white photograph taken five years earlier of a

South Vietnamese police captain shooting an insurgent in the head. As the dead Vietnamese, as well as the people inside the burning house, were our enemies, it was not necessary to pity them. When I read that Patty Hearst had not been in the house, I was relieved.

Dick and I bought a big Spanish-style house on Outpost Drive in Hollywood that had been built in the Thirties for Dolores Del Rio by her husband, the production designer Cedric Gibbons. The front door led to a hall with a tiled staircase leading to a living room with French doors opening into the garden. The ceiling was twenty-five feet high, carved and painted in the style of a Spanish gallery. There was an acre of overgrown garden with a brick fishpond and fountain, and a swimming pool. The house was ravishing, Gibbons having wanted to please his wife with unusual architectural details and flourishes. I went to work in the garden, making a long allée of white camellia trees, and a hillside of iris and allium, helped each day by a crew of good-humored Hispanic men sent from the studio by Dick. I soon realized that he had added the cost of the trees and other plantings, as well as that of the men's labor, to the budget of some film, and although I knew that this was stealing, I said nothing and asked for more plants— lavender water lilies for the pond, hedges of philadelphus, clematis *jackmanii* and *lanuginosa*, thirty agapanthus plants, and two jacaranda trees.

Over the years, Dick had bought good pieces of eighteenth-century French provincial furniture, including a dining table and chairs, as well as nineteenth-century English and American paintings and drawings, and these arrived from storage in New York. As for the rest of the decoration, he asked if I would do it, which was flattering and even generous, given his very particular aesthetic. When I was finished, he was pleased with it. Soon after everything was at last in place, Josie and Peter Davis came to dinner. We sat in the garden, then went inside, where she wandered in astonishment through the beautiful rooms. "I swear to God," she said to Dick in admiration, "my next husband is going to be a designer." Dick thanked her, and I was silent.

Marriage, to my surprise, had not made me feel safe, but the opposite. For the first time in my life, I was intensely jealous, convinced that Dick would leave me for another woman. He was in the world, after all, surrounded by amusing people of talent and beauty, and I was in the garden, planting bulbs. Although he had never shown an interest in other women during our time together, and was, except for sex, devoted to me, I told myself that he would not be able to resist the heady enticements of the glamorous women with whom he often worked. When Dick was working on *The Fortune*, a movie directed by Mike with Warren and Jack and Stockard Channing, I thought I saw Stockard kissing him in the sunroom on Outpost Drive—I couldn't be sure, and he later seemed perplexed by my accusation. My jealousy frightened me and I decided that I needed some help. I began to see an analyst in Beverly Hills three days a week.

He sat behind me and, in what was clearly a tribute to Freud, I lay on a brown leather daybed with a heavy paisley lap rug at my feet. I had chosen a traditional psychoanalyst, even though they were out of fashion, because I did not want consolation, which I knew was not offered in Freudian analysis. When I told him about my nightmare, he said that I suffered from a condition known as pavor nocturnus, or sleep terrors. The dream sometimes appeared within minutes of my falling asleep, and he encouraged me to keep a journal next to my bed in which I could record the time of the attacks, which sometimes occurred two and three times a night. He told me that my nightmare did not exist apart from me, as I insisted, but *was* me, an idea that I found irritating. He asked if I had suffered sexual abuse in childhood and had buried the memory of it. My dream, he thought, might be an attempt to recall what had happened to me. I was able to assure him that any trauma I suffered in childhood had not been overtly sexual.

Over the year that I saw him, I gleaned what seemed to me, given that I saw his face for only a few seconds at the beginning and end of a session, a compelling dossier of information about him, much of it determined by smell and sound. As closely as he listened to me, or so I hoped, I listened to him, trying to discern the level of his interest or boredom by the frequency of his sighs and the scratch of his pen in his notebook. He did not smoke. He had seasonal allergies and used a handkerchief to blow his nose rather than pull tissues from a box. He sometimes sucked discreetly on a lozenge. He now and then, politely although unsuccessfully, attempted to swallow a yawn. He did not, to my relief, wear scent. He used Head & Shoulders shampoo, a smell that I recognized, as Dick used it, too, which led me to believe that he had dandruff, an assumption supported by the sound of his hand brushing the shoulders of his tweed jacket. There were occasional complaints from his stomach, but as my session was at noon, he may have been hungry rather than dyspeptic. His shoes had rubber soles. He kept his eyeglasses, used for taking notes, in a hinged case that made a loud snap when he closed it at the end of our session, having removed his glasses and shifted in his seat.

During our time together, he gave me a few hints in the hope, I suspect, that I would better understand and perhaps even forgive myself. "Thank God your mother loved you," he said.

ONE DAY IN the spring of 1957, when I was eleven years old, my mother disappeared. My brothers and sister and I searched the house, under the beds and in the closets, but she was gone. We waited in the road for our father to come home from work, and rushed to his car when he turned into the driveway. All he would say was that our mother had not been feeling well, and had been taken to a very nice place where she would soon be made whole again, which caused my brother Michael to think that she had been taken apart at the arms and legs and thrown into the ocean.

Each afternoon after school, we took to our bicycles to find her, searching the neighborhood in ever-widening circles as I had been taught to do in the Brownies when lost, but we did not find her, and after a week, we stopped looking for her. In the endless days and nights that followed, we abandoned ourselves to the deepest grief. Where could she be? Who would tell us the truth?

A few weeks after my mother's disappearance, my father sent for me, and I rushed to the library in the hope that he would tell me that she was on her way home to us. He was sitting at the desk made of native koa wood that was said to have belonged to the high chiefess Princess Ruth. There were papers on the desk, along with medical journals, books, and the heavy black telephone I had used to call the police when the house was under attack. I was surprised to feel flecks of what looked like wood shavings under my bare feet.

The house in Tantalus where Princess Ruth's desk was defaced

My father pointed to a drawer of the desk, where I saw, carved deeply into the wood, my name, Susan Paine Moore, in capital letters. I was very shocked. It would have taken some time and care to form the words with such precision, and it would have required dexterity. I lowered myself to the floor to give myself time to think, fitting my fingers into the letters of my name. I'd been reading *The Count of Monte Cristo* and had an exaggerated reverence for titled ladies of any nation or color, so that a desk once used by a princess, even so unlikely a princess as a fierce-looking Hawaiian woman of almost three hundred pounds, was a hallowed object. The thought that someone had ruined Princess Ruth's desk by carving my name into it only added to my sense of alarm, especially as I knew, even if my father did not, that I was for once absolved of the misery of deceit and would not need the small lies of childhood that serve as protection against the seemingly arbitrary demands set by adults. I also knew that if he chose not to believe me, it would make my supposed crime even worse, in that I'd ruined the desk and then lied about it.

I told him that I did not do it.

"Because," he said slowly, offering me his hand to pull me to my feet, "you are a child who does not lie, I will—despite what is here in front of us—believe you." He sounded a little disappointed, whether in my innocence or in the fact that our family harbored a vandal, I couldn't tell. I was relieved to be let off so easily, but also troubled. I had already begun to understand, thanks in part to my reading, that extreme situations tend to reveal character, if only for a moment or two. But was I really a child who did not lie? I wasn't convinced. And if I were that child, what an enormous burden such rectitude would be.

I was interested by the ease with which my father was willing to believe me. I knew that he was, at best, detached, the perfect radiologist, each day deciphering the black-and-white X-ray images that served as reminders of the disembodiment that awaited us all, rarely touching or even seeing a patient in the flesh, a diagnostician consulted by his fellow physicians. He had chosen a medical specialty in which he did not need to offer solace, or even explanation. His ample charm would not be wasted on strangers whom he had no wish to seduce. My mother had told me that he decided to become a doctor when, as a boy, he learned that his mother had suddenly been stricken with a mysterious paralysis that left her unable to move her legs, an affliction that lasted for the rest of her life, and one which my father did not believe was real.

A few days after he called me to the library, Ishi, the gardener, having left his rubber tabis in the kitchen, padded barefoot through the house to the library carrying his homemade wooden toolbox. I stood behind him and watched as he sanded away my name, letter by letter.

Not long after the night of the desk, when my mother was still missing, my father asked if I would like to go with him to a *National Geographic* slide show on New Guinea at the local high school. I ran to my room to wet my hair and spent a frustrating ten minutes trying to tamp down the cowlick at the back of my head. I wore one of my mother's embroidered cashmere cardigans, taken from her closet, where I had been spending quite a bit of time, and I wondered if he would recognize that it belonged to her. It certainly smelled like her.

I hoped that he had invited me because he liked my company, but it is more likely that in his restlessness and boredom he simply wanted something to do, and didn't want to show up at the high school auditorium alone. There were not many things to do in Honolulu in 1957, where a *National Geographic* travelogue was considered a cultural event. It is also possible that he was meeting someone there.

After school each day, I would help Ishi in the large garden, which extended down the side of a hill to an abandoned swimming pool. Sometimes the other children would accompany us, especially when it was time to gather liliko'i, or passion fruit, from the vines that grew along the old stone walls.

Ishi, who was in his seventies, suffered from rheumatism. As it was difficult for him to climb the rickety bamboo ladder in the orchard, I was given the job of collecting Tahitian limes from the trees at the bottom of the hill.

One rainy afternoon, we sat under a monkeypod tree to share his lunch of Spam sushi, tamago, and daikon. He leaned against the trunk of the tree and I sat on his lap, holding his tin bento box. As I began to arrange our lunch on the indigo napkin he kept inside the box, he slipped his hand down the front of my shorts and rested it between my legs, touching that part of me that I had been taught was not meant to be touched by anyone, including me. The air around us grew still. I turned to look at him and saw that he was crying. I pulled his hand from my shorts, the elastic waistband snapping softly against my stomach. I lifted myself from his lap, overturning the food into the grass, and walked to the house. I called my father at the hospital. I will be home in a few minutes, he said.

I waited on the screened sleeping porch, which overlooked the garden. I could hear my brothers and sister in the playroom, and the sound of the radio in the kitchen. I felt as if I were underwater, moving without haste, my arms and legs heavy as I leaned against the current. Then I saw my father, still wearing his white coat. Ishi emerged from a grove of bamboo and pulled his torn straw hat from his head. Oh! I thought. I have never seen you without your hat, Ishi. You are losing your hair!

He glanced once at the house, and then turned and walked away. My father waited as he disappeared down the hill, then he, too, looked toward the house. Later that evening, my father said that he was proud of me. I knew that I was not to blame, but I also knew that I had lost my beloved Ishi. He had not harmed me other than to teach me that there is no sureness, no certainty in love. I never saw him again, no one ever saw him again, although for a number of years, he left baskets of orchids on the kitchen steps each Sunday morning before sunrise.

Not long after, I came home from school to find my mother sitting in the garden—really sitting in the garden, not in my imagination. I ran across the lawn and threw myself into her lap, knocking her to the ground, where she held me in her arms until we both stopped crying. She said that she had been taken to the state mental hospital in Kāne'ohe, thirty miles away, where she had been forced to undergo electric shock treatments. When she saw me staring at the side of her head, little spikes of hair just beginning to appear where it had been shaved, she said, "That is where they attach the electrodes.

My mother and father on the beach at the Outrigger Canoe Club, Waikiki, 1956

They did it so I would forget, but I didn't forget." She held her shaking hands to her face. Her right cheek had been rubbed raw. "Don't tell anyone," she whispered, and I promised that I would not tell. My mother had been replaced by a ghost.

I sensed that my father's infidelity, despite his promises to my mother that he had ended his affair, was the cause of her increasing instability, and there were times when my anger was so great that I could not sleep. One night, not long after she returned, I rushed into the garden, shouting that I could not stand it any longer, only to be chased by my father, who caught me and led me back to the house. Later, when she was dead, I wrote him a long accusatory letter. He did not acknowledge that he had received it, and I wondered if I had done myself and my brothers and sisters more harm than if I had remained silent. It was impossible to know.

Much later, I learned that it was not my mother's first nervous collapse. My Aunt Pat, much given to sorrowful revelations that she perhaps should have kept to herself, told me that my mother had twice been to Kāne'ohe, once before my father's affair, when she was thirty years old. It had happened when she was pregnant with her fifth child. A few weeks before the baby was due, she went into labor in the middle of the night. We were hurried across the lawn by the maid and left with a neighbor, who put us in her guest room, two to a bed. As my aunt spoke, I remembered that as soon as my brothers and sisters had fallen asleep, I went to a window from which I could see the light in my parents' bedroom. My aunt said that my father had called an ambulance, but it had not come in time and he delivered the child himself, a perfectly formed boy. It was a difficult birth and the baby was deprived of oxygen for the few seconds it took my father to revive him. My mother and the baby were taken to the hospital, but the baby, who had suffered minor brain damage during the delivery, died that morning. My mother was heartbroken. In an attempt to console her, a nurse said that it must have been a difficult decision for Dr. Moore, although she was sure he'd done the right thing. My mother was so shocked, so stricken that she could not speak. She would have kept the child, but my father, without her knowledge and knowing that she would have never consented, had allowed the baby to die. "That was the beginning," my aunt said.

I WANTED VERY MUCH to have a child, but thought that it might not be possible, given the infrequency of sex with my husband. When I told him that I would like to have a baby, he was surprised, but he did not discourage me. I did everything that might help me to conceive, including the purchase of alluring nightgowns, and the perhaps equally ineffective trick of standing on my head after intercourse. I took my temperature daily so as to keep track of my ovulation cycle. To my amazement, I became pregnant. My mother had told me that she craved oranges when she was pregnant with me, so I wanted oranges, too. Dick painted my portrait, a dark-eyed, solemn young woman with a Louise Brooks haircut.

One night in July, soon after I'd learned that I was pregnant, Mike Nichols telephoned and asked to speak to me, which was unusual. He was calling to tell me that Josie Davis had been killed that afternoon, hit by a taxi while she stood with her son on the corner of Charles Street in the West Village. Her son was not hurt. On his way home, Peter had noticed the police cars and ambulance on Charles Street and thought that perhaps Patty Hearst had at last been caught. He learned that Josie was dead when a woman came up to him on the street holding a pair of trousers. She said that if they were his, it must have been his wife who was taking them to the cleaners when she was killed.

Although I could not carry a tune, it seemed extremely important after Josie's death that I learn to play a musical instrument, preferably the cello. I found in the phone book the name of a teacher and I went to see her. Mrs. Humphreys gave music lessons in a derelict Victorian house that she owned on Yucca Street, north of Hollywood Boulevard. She told me as soon as I stepped onto the sagging porch that in the Forties the house had been a rooming house for young actresses. I could tell from the absence of any students, although the stacks of yellowing sheet music, and the pile of bows that I at first took for kindling, suggested their presence in the past, that Mrs. Humphreys would be happy to take me as a pupil, even though I could not read music. She even had an old cello that I could use. She herself, she told me, had once been a cellist in the orchestra of a big midwestern city.

We spent the first fifteen minutes of my lesson chatting as she tuned her cello and then my cello, and tightened and rosined our bows. Sometimes she would pull a scrapbook from inside the piano bench to show me photographs of herself as a young woman, standing next to her cello, her hand around its neck. She took our lessons seriously, even though it was soon apparent that I would never play the cello. Once, to tease her, I asked how long it would be before I could play the Brahms cello sonatas, and she said, without a hint of humor, "Oh, my dear, forty years at least." I stopped seeing her soon after, not that I was discouraged, but because I had reached the ninth month of my pregnancy and could no longer hold the cello.

I could see that I caused Dick and some of my friends, although not Joan, to worry when I bought baby clothes for a girl and made a list of girls' names. When they cautiously warned that I might have a boy, I assured them that there was no reason for concern. I held on to this fantasy until the end, never doubting it, when, to everyone's relief, I gave birth at the end of March to a girl. Her name is Lulu. Her godparents are Joan and Roman, an unsettling combination so illustrative of the period, according to Joan, that she wrote in *The White Album*, "Quite often I reflect on the big house in Hollywood . . . and on the fact that Roman Polanski and I are godparents to the same child, but writing has not yet helped me see what it means."

My father wrote that he had heard I had a baby, who was his first grandchild. We had not spoken in ten years. He enclosed a pretty gold baby bracelet from Tiffany, which I immediately lost, although I did write to thank him. I was aware that the strength of will required in order to remain angry at him, enraged really, was not something that I could afford to spare, but I couldn't help myself. It seemed easiest to keep as far from him and my stepmother as possible.

Many years later, the writer Brian Moore told me that it was quite obvious that Joan's new book, *Democracy*, which he had just read in manuscript, was about me and my sister Tina, as the main characters were two young women who'd grown up in Hawai'i. I was quite flattered, and naively asked Joan if it was true. She did not answer me, as I should have expected. When I read the book, I was both relieved and disappointed to discover that the story had nothing to do with me or my sister. I'd once told Joan that my mother kept us home from school at the slightest whim, once in order to teach us to paint our nails, and a version of this is in Joan's book, but that is all. When I told my sister, reminding her that our mother had taught us to paint our nails, she interrupted me to whisper, "It was me! It was me!" When I looked confused, she shook me by the shoulders. "I carved your name in Princess Ruth's desk. I did it." In my astonishment, I remembered that it was my sister, adept with tools, as well as meticulous, who had taught me to paint my nails, not my mother. "I did it," she said again, and burst into tears.

BOB EVANS, who was the head of Paramount Pictures, asked Dick to be vice president in charge of production at Paramount. As Dick had no formal experience in studio production, people were surprised, including Dick himself, but he accepted the job. It was an eccentric, even perverse decision on Bob's part to choose an aloof intellectual and artist to run a movie company for profit, and it was not clear why he had made such an unusual appointment.

Suddenly our life became more glamorous. I began to dress in Saint Laurent, buying pieces as I could afford them from the Rive Gauche boutique in Beverly Hills, silk blouses, cotton sailor's pants, a black velvet suit with jet buttons and a mandarin collar, and brightly colored poplin shirts cut like smocks. There was an enormous expense account, and parties to give, including a dinner in the garden at Outpost for Richard Burton and Elizabeth Taylor, for which I hired a mariachi band. The Burtons were fond of Dick, having become friends a few years earlier when he was the production designer of *Who's Afraid of Virginia Woolf?* Both Elizabeth and Dick had won Academy Awards for the film, and she was always a bit emotional when she saw him. There were new friends like the Italian director Antonioni, who came to dinner with his silent young girlfriend, Clare Peploe. The producer Jerry Bick brought Dick a screenplay about the women who worked in factories during the Second World War, and through Jerry, who was also a book collector, I met his wife, Louise Fletcher. I invited my brother Rick to every party, and sometimes he would come, tall and handsome and reserved, and the day after the party some of the women would ask me about him when they called to thank me. Buck Henry often came to dinner with his beautiful and witty English girlfriend, Fiona Lewis. He had not been particularly interested in me when we first met in Abaco, even a bit chilly, but he changed his mind about me and we became close. He subscribed in my name to a number of pornographic magazines, which shocked Dick when he found them on the hall table where the housekeeper left them once she had read them and before I had a chance to throw them away.

Despite Dick's new job, we were not included in the more exclusive circle of Hollywood executives and agents who revolved around Sue Mengers, David Geffen, and Barry Diller. We were asked to one dinner at Mengers' house. I was seated at a round table across from a dress designer, who leaned toward her dinner partner and, looking at me, asked in a loud voice, "Who *is* that?" After that, I was relieved not to be included, and would have refused an invitation had it been offered. To be part of this set would have been beneficial to Dick's career and would have made his work easier, especially if he wished to remain an executive at Paramount, but there was not much that we could do about it short of obsequity, something at which neither of us excelled.

The writer and director Joel Schumacher,
Los Angeles, 1974

I wondered if it might help me to write if I took some classes, and I applied to UCLA as a first-year student, telling no one. I was so restless, so eager to do something of interest and worth that I allowed myself to be convinced by my friend Joel Schumacher, as well as by Jack, to take an acting class. Jack suggested that I see Jeff Corey, a former actor who began teaching in the Fifties when he was blacklisted. Over the years, he had taught many notable actors, including Jack himself. Although I knew that I was not an actor, I went to see him in the vague hope that an acting class might lead to something else. I was accepted immediately and without the usual audition, mainly, I understood, because Dick might someday be of use to him. The class met twice a week in a studio in the San Fernando Valley. There were a dozen people in the class, most of them younger than me, including a boyish actor named Dennis Quaid. It was immediately clear that he was the only one with any talent. He knew it, too, and sat with me in the back row of tiered seats, pretending to be bored and embarrassed when in truth he was, unlike me, alert and intent. It was so obvious that the rest of us were wasting our time, or worse, wasting Jeff Corey's time, not that Mr. Corey seemed to mind, that it was dispiriting to feel complicit in what more and more seemed like a lie. If I knew that none of us, other than Dennis, would ever be actors, Mr. Corey surely knew it. I stopped attending the class after a few sessions. Years later when I was teaching young men recently released from Rikers Island, I remembered my acting class. I was helping my students learn enough of the basics to obtain a high school diploma, an unlikely achievement held out to them, although not by me, as the guaranteed means to just about everything—a job, money, a career, even a college education. Of course it was helpful to have a high school degree in order to find a job, but many of the boys could barely read or write, and

Anthea Sylbert and Lulu, Los Angeles, 1975

it seemed dishonest, and even dangerous, given their inevitable disappointment, to deceive them. I felt the same ambivalence, although in a milder way, when later I taught creative writing at a university.

A dignified Creole woman from Belize named Sonia came to work for us at Outpost. Although she was only a few years older than me, she taught me how to be a mother. We would watch *Soul Train* while I breastfed the baby, both of us mesmerized by the unctuous Don Cornelius. In April, we watched the evacuation by helicopter of the American embassy in Saigon, men clinging to the landing skids of the helicopters as they ascended, the helicopters shuddering under the weight of too many passengers.

Sonia taught me how to talk to my nightmare or, as my analyst would have it, to myself. Awakened one night by my screams, she followed me into the garden the following morning to ask if I'd seen a ghost man. When I explained that I'd had a bad dream, she said that before going to sleep, I had to shout at my dream, daring it to come after me, and warn it that it would be impossible to catch me. I was relieved that she, too, saw the dream as a malignant spirit separate from me. That night, I did as she said, and while my dream did not run away in fright, it caused me less terror than usual. From then on, I did everything that Sonia told me to do.

I often overheard her warn Lulu that if she did not take care, Jackie Vasquez would steal her away. I began to worry about this Jackie Vasquez, even if Lulu was still too young to take fright herself. When I asked Sonia about him, she said that he had first appeared during her grandmother's time, wearing a round black hat, baggy pants that reached his knees, and wooden shoes. Jackie Vasquez abducted children, and if there were no children around, he took men and women. For generations, mothers had warned their children that if they misbehaved, Jackie Vasquez would catch them. I wondered if Jackie Vasquez could be the folk memory of a Spanish slave trader. As Sonia believed in him without question, I hesitated to ask her, and it was weeks before I told her my theory. She looked at me in disappointment, and said, "He's the slave man. I thought you knew that. He's in your dream."

I was happy with my baby. Dick was a tender and attentive father, and her half brothers were enthralled by her. She was what my grandmother called a good baby, owlish, placid, easily amused. Now and then I thought that I might someday write the story of my childhood for her, in the hope that it would help her to understand how I had come to be her mother. Although I'd been accepted at UCLA as a freshman, I'd begun to think that writing was something I could do on my own, without the benefit of a freshman writing class. Still, my notebooks remained on the table next to my bed, opened only when I had something to add to them.

Dick went to Paramount each morning, having approved the financing of the movies *Bugsy Malone*, in which children, including a young Jodie Foster, danced and sang, and *Looking for Mr. Goodbar*, with Diane Keaton, two projects that could not have been more disparate in style and content. In the spring of 1976, we went to France. I had met Gerald Van der Kemp, an art historian and the man responsible for the restoration of Versailles, at Connie's house, and when I told her that I would be in Paris, she wrote to him. M. Van der Kemp mistakenly thought that I was someone to be indulged, thanks to Dick's position rather than, as had happened in the past, to Ale Kaiser's beautiful clothes, and he arranged that I spend a day at Versailles when it was not open to the public, accompanied by an historian whose knowledge of the seventeenth century was, according to M. Van der Kemp, *inégalée*. It was, as may be imagined, a most extraordinary day. The historian told me that the ladies of the palace had assumed a particular mincing walk in their high heels, tiptoeing across the parquet in quick little steps, almost but not quite running, and he allowed me to try it in the Gallerie des Batailles, to little effect. I knew that M. Van der Kemp was hoping for a donation to the Versailles Foundation from Paramount, which was unfortunately not forthcoming, and he must have been disappointed by the exorbitant basket of flowers that I asked the Ritz to send him. As I had learned in the past, it would have been better to have the money.

Sitting with Dick, Isabelle Adjani, and the cinematographer
Sven Nykvist at a party in the South of France given by
Adnan Khashoggi, Cannes, 1976

Dick and I went to Antibes, staying at the Hotel du Cap in order to attend the Cannes Film Festival. Vicky Tiel, a dress designer, came from Paris to see us. Polanski was in Cannes, and my friend Johnny Pigozzi was in residence at his nearby villa. Marcel Ophüls, who had made the documentary *The Sorrow and the Pity*, was showing his new film, *The Memory of Justice*, out of competition at the festival. One afternoon at lunch, I met Ophüls and his young producer, an American named Hamilton Fish, at Pigozzi's house, and I saw Ham a few

With Hamilton Fish at Johnny Pigozzi's house,
Cap d'Antibes, 1976

nights later at a party given by the Saudi arms dealer Adnan Khashoggi, where I noticed the presence of so many beautiful women, among them a number of clearly teenage girls, that I asked about them. Roman, who was there, told me that the girls had been sent from Paris by Mme Claude to accommodate Khashoggi's guests.

At dinner, I sat between the Swedish cinematographer Sven Nykvist and Ham, who told me that he had recently moved to New York after graduating from Harvard. He said that he wanted to do work that was both artistic and intellectual and, most important of all, work that would serve to expose injustice. What could be better? I wondered. Money, perhaps, but I had never thought about money. It was as if I had at last found the boy whom I was meant to love, only I was thirty years old with a husband and a baby and lived in Los Angeles.

At the end of the party, I decided, as a way to prolong the evening, that I wanted to swim. Dick didn't swim—I had never seen him in a bathing suit—and he was tired and wanted to go to bed, but Ham thought that a midnight swim would be the perfect way to end the night and he returned with us to the hotel. Dick said goodnight and Ham and I walked through the dark garden to the hotel's swimming pool overlooking the Mediterranean. There were no lights at the pool. It was surrounded by a fence on three sides and the fence gate was locked. I took off my evening dress and shoes and climbed the fence, pleased to see that Ham was following me. We slipped into the water, careful not to touch each other, so aware of our overwhelming wish to touch each other that we began to shout with laughter. Afraid that we might be heard by a night watchman, we calmed ourselves and climbed back over the fence and dried ourselves with our clothes before dressing. He held my hand and we walked to the hotel, where I hurried past the dozing desk clerk to my room.

Home in Los Angeles, I could think only of Hamilton. I thought, too, about the many steps and missteps that had taken me to France. Every possibility had been awakened in me. The fear that I sometimes felt quietly disappeared, replaced by a radiance that might, if I were not to squander it, withstand my constant grief. In some ways, Ham was the least of it.

I couldn't tell anyone. I couldn't even tell Ham. Instead, I wrote him a flirtatious letter, not too serious, not too compromising, and one that allowed him the freedom not to answer me. He wrote to me immediately, many letters, several a week, and I wrote back to him. Because I knew that I could trust Sonia to look after Lulu, I told Dick that I was going to New York for a few days, where I would stay at Candy Bergen's empty apartment on Central Park South. Dick must have thought this sudden trip a bit odd, especially as I had not traveled alone since our marriage, but he said nothing.

Hamilton was waiting for me outside the door of Candy's apartment, and he did not leave me for the next four days. I had never been so happy. We had dinner one night with Mike and Annabel, and although I had not told her about Hamilton, she whispered to me, "This is how I always imagined you might be." Despite my elation, I had no expectations, no plan, no thought that I would leave Dick. No fantasy that Ham would move to Los Angeles. All the same, something had happened.

Lulu with her great-grandmother, Mae Shields, Los Angeles, 1975

I returned to Outpost Drive and my long, peaceful days with Sonia and my beloved Lulu. Two of Dick's sons were visiting during their summer vacation, and each day we sat by the pool with the baby to play cards and listen to music. Hamilton and I continued to write, but we did not know when we would see each other again. Now and then, I wondered if Dick knew that I had been with Ham. He was often impatient with me and with his sons, which I decided was caused by the stress that he must feel in his job. I was teaching his son Mark to drive my 1962 blue Studebaker, and one afternoon when I thought that Mark had turned off the engine, he accelerated by mistake and crashed through the garage doors, badly damaging them, and causing the stucco supports at the side of the garage to crumble into pieces, endangering the foundation of the house. Dick was angry out of all proportion, and I again wondered if he might know about Hamilton. He complained about the expense it would be to repair the damage. Even though I knew that he would simply send over some men from the studio to do the work and that he would not be billed, I offered to pay for the repairs and he accepted my offer. Now, I, too, was furious.

I knew that I was not about to run away with Ham, but I also knew that everything was not well between Dick and myself. His sense of grievance, his certainty that he was not getting his due, had not been eased by the importance of his new job. I knew that if he was troubled about our marriage, or jealous, or hurt, he would not be able to tell me so, and I asked him if he was upset with me. No, he said. I asked if we could see a therapist together. No, he said, why would I want to do that? When I asked if he remembered what it was like to love me, he was silent, even though I knew that he did remember. I had a sense of his presence, his dark oily hair, never washed enough for my liking, his thumb stained with tobacco, his dashing eyes, his full mouth held in a tight intractable line. If with the birth of my child, I had come to feel that I myself was no longer the child, that I was no longer in need of a parent, he was not to blame. I did not know if I had the means or the will to fix things. In the end, I had not tended to him, and he had not tended to me.

———

FOR THE LONGEST TIME, I believed that my mother committed suicide. There was no evidence or even suggestion that she
had—no distress or violence the night of her death, no note, no
overturned pill bottles, no untidy bullet hole in the side of her
head. Her obituary noted that she had recently been treated
for a nervous condition, which quickly led to gossip that she
had been emotionally unstable. It was true, but I did not want
all of Honolulu to know it. My father said that she died of
arteriosclerosis, which is quite unusual in a woman thirty-five
years old. The older sister of a school friend told me excitedly
that people wondered if my father had killed her, a rumor so
offensive that I did not give it another thought. My father did
not kill my mother.

When my father was very old and I was speaking to him for
the first time as a grown woman about my mother, he said that
one of his few regrets—one could have wished for more—was
that he had not allowed an autopsy of her body. He'd awakened that morning in June to find her dead beside him. They
had been to a party the night before. She'd worn a gold dress,
bought in Philadelphia, and a dark purple velvet jacket with
gold buttons. I knew this because she'd asked me a few days
earlier, not without a wry awareness that her need to be admired was as great as her need to be accepted, if I thought
her dress, a sleeveless brocade sheath, the armholes cut high
under the arm, too fancy for the party. The grandees of Honolulu society, provincial and snobbish, wore oversized silk aloha
shirts and flowered mu'umu'us on the most formal of occasions,

but my mother, who was tall and slender, was not well suited, temperamentally as well as physically, to loose nightgown-like dresses in bright patterns.

I'd spent the night of the party with my best friend, Penny Oliver, who lived almost an hour away in Mānoa Valley. The phone rang early Sunday morning at the Olivers' house, waking me. I waited for someone to answer it, but Penny's parents and the other children were still asleep, and I was relieved when the ringing stopped abruptly. When the phone rang a second time, I ran into the kitchen to answer it, surprised to hear my sister's voice. For a moment, I wondered how she could possibly have the Olivers' number. She whispered, "Mama stopped breathing," and hung up. When I called back, the phone was answered by a policeman, familiar to me from the neighborhood, primarily as the finder of lost dogs. I asked to speak to my mother. When he said, "I think you'd better come home," I knew that she was dead.

I went into Mr. and Mrs. Oliver's bedroom to wake them. They dressed quickly, startled and worried. I was grateful that they did not ask any questions, but accepted without hesitation my demand that they take me home. I did not tell them that my mother was dead, only that something bad had happened and that I had to leave at once. No one spoke during the drive across the island to Portlock. I sat in the back seat with the window down and my head out the window, my eyes closed.

When we reached Portlock, there was a coroner's truck in the driveway and a police car. The thought that my mother was in the truck was unbearable to me, and I ran past it and into the house. My brothers and sisters, frightened and confused, were in the playroom with a neighbor. I went into my parents' bedroom. There was nothing amiss, nothing out of place, nothing to indicate that she had died there.

The room still held her smell, a mixture of Chanel No. 5 and carnation-scented soap. Her red Chinese slippers were next to the bed, and a book, *Bonjour Tristesse*, was on her bedside table. The bedsheets were warm, the pillows thrown aside. I sat on the edge of the bed, arranging myself with care as I fitted myself into the impression left by her body. That she had died alone, my father and brothers and sisters already lost to her in sleep, made me so sad that for a moment I could not breathe. As I lay there, I could hear my father in the next room, where he was on the telephone. He was crying and found it difficult to speak. "I loved her so much, Mother. I loved her so much," I heard him say. And I thought, Maybe you did.

In order to distract us and to get us out of the way, my brothers and sisters and I were dropped at the Honolulu Zoo in Waikiki, half an hour away. The zoo was a dry and dusty place, barely inhabited save for a few depressed spider monkeys, an aged camel pocked with mange, and hundreds of feral chickens who roamed freely through the zoo, tormenting the other animals. As it was still early, we were the only humans there. Perhaps there were other visitors later, but I did not see them as we wandered from cage to cage. I'd been given a few dollars to buy sodas, but the concession stand was not yet open, and I used them to buy peanuts and a box of Raisinets from a vending machine, half of which we ate before throwing what was left to the monkeys.

As the day went by, I began to wonder if we had been forgotten. It was very hot, and the younger children were tired and irritable. My brother, who had been pushing the baby in a stroller for hours, refused to take another step. We sat for a long time on a bench, as dazed and as dirty as the monkeys, now and then stumbling to a nearby drinking fountain to ease our throats with warm water. It was then that I first had the sensation of watching myself, transported like one of my favorite fairy-tale characters, the Goose Girl perhaps, to a place unknown to me where overwhelming tasks awaited me. I could not understand how our mother could have left us, knowing how much she loved us. I was sure of that, that we had been loved, but this only added to my confusion.

I was certain, too, that I could have saved her, had I only been at home. This was not simply the fantasy of omnipotence that children of troubled parents tend to nurture as consolation for their inexhaustible distress. In the two years before her death, when I was ten and eleven years old, she had tried to kill herself several times. I had never allowed myself to believe that my mother really intended to die on those grotesque occasions, and I'd told myself that they were gestures of desperation, intended to win my father's sympathy. Her despair grew more extreme with each failure. It was not working, could not possibly work, in small part because I refused to ask my father for help, perhaps because I was intent on saving her myself. I threw pills into the toilet, locked her in her room, and once, to my shock, knocked her to the ground. The misleading sense of power that I could not help but feel was dangerous for us both, but I was too young and too frightened to know better, and there was no one to tell me otherwise.

Toward closing time, a friend of my mother's was sent to find us at the zoo, coming across us on our bench, where she was so alarmed by our appearance that she took us to the Hawaiian

Village Hotel, where we could swim and have something to eat. When my brother Rick, sitting at the edge of the hotel's pool, his legs in the water, whispered to the attendant that his mother had died that morning, the man shouted loudly, *"You're doing cannonballs and your mother just died?"* My brother left the pool to hide in the changing room, so ashamed that he only told me of it fifty years later.

I WOKE ONE MORNING to feed Lulu, and to my surprise found myself in the room where Dick made his flies, the baby in my arms. I told him that I wanted to go away for a while. "Where are you thinking you might go?" he asked, his eyes on the delicate feathers held between his thumb and forefinger. I said that I didn't know. I wished to be alone for a little while. He reminded me that I was alone much of the day, and I said that I meant something else. I wanted to live alone with Lulu, nearby and not separated, but apart. I could see that he was startled, how could he not be, but he said nothing. He did not ask where I would go, or what I would do for money, which made me angry, and because of that, it did not occur to me that he was too wounded to ask me anything.

A friend had an empty apartment in Beverly Hills, near my first apartment on Charleville, which he invited me to use while he was abroad, and I arranged with the gardener at Outpost to take apart Lulu's crib and to bring it to the apartment along with my notebooks and two suitcases. I left everything else behind, intending to return in a few weeks' time. Sonia would help me with the baby every morning. I was still reading scripts for Jack, still earning one hundred and fifty dollars a week, which I would give to Sonia.

I told no one where I was living. I knew that my wish to be alone had nothing to do with Hamilton, whom I reassured, unwilling to trouble him. I sensed that Dick would be willing to overlook any bad behavior on my part, even sexual betrayal, and that I could continue to see Hamilton if that was what I wanted, but I had no desire to be that girl. I didn't want to be like my father. I took no particular pleasure in betrayal. I was thirty years old, and should have found a wiser, even more practical way to mend my marriage, but I was not thinking clearly. As in the past, I had no one to tell me that I was behaving impetuously, or even sensibly, for that matter. John and Joan did not at first know where to find me, but when they at last tracked me down, Joan said she was not surprised that I had disappeared, as I had spent my life running away, a thought that did not please me, especially as I had no wish to run away.

Bushes of calycanthus grew outside the bedroom window, their dark red flowers heavy with scent, and it was difficult to sleep. Lulu cried in her new room, her crib squeezed between a bookcase and a window. On the weekends when Sonia was not with us, I took her to a park in Beverly Hills, where I noticed that there were very few women, the children accompanied by men who were, I assumed, either divorced or unusually attentive fathers.

I learned from John Dunne that a few days after I'd left, a friend of mine who had always claimed to be in love with Dick had moved into the house on Outpost Drive. That Dick could manage to be interested in another woman was bad enough, but that a friend could be so disloyal was shocking to me. As I had been the one to ask to live apart, if only for a short time, I had the mistaken idea that I had no right to insist that Dick behave as if I still lived with him, although it had never occurred to me that another woman would immediately move into my house. I wondered if she wore my clothes and read the books next to my bed and sat in my iris garden. I was very upset, but I said nothing. That I had slept with Hamilton made it seem only fair that Dick could sleep with whomever he liked, even if he did not know about Hamilton. Those were my thoughts, shaped by pride and guilt.

A week after John told me that my friend had moved in with Dick, I answered the door to discover an embarrassed-looking summons server, who handed me an envelope before hurrying down the walkway. What a terrible job, I thought, as I opened the envelope. I was to be divorced. My friend had gone through my things and found the letters that Hamilton had written me, and showed them to Dick. I would, it seemed, be sent away for good. This has happened to me before, I thought, but the first time, my grandmother and my aunt had been waiting for me.

I could have fought for him, and won, but I turned away from him. I would leave Los Angeles, taking Lulu and a few belongings and my notebooks. I would leave everything else behind, to be collected at some other time, or perhaps not.

I understood at last that I had not intended to abandon my brothers and sisters when I left them that summer in Honolulu. I had not intended anything. I would never know how my mother died, but I no longer thought that she had killed herself. Perhaps it was an accident. Perhaps she was ill, as my father claimed. I no longer thought that I was like her, too fragile, too crazy to survive. Her continuous dying had exhausted me, and

I wondered if the secret desire of the mournful is to be guilty while innocent. I still had many questions to which there were as yet no answers.

I would find a place to live. And a real job. That was something I could do. It would be all right.

Unless otherwise noted, all photographs are courtesy of the author:

page 31: Henry J. Kaiser and Alyce Chester: Maurice Mitchell.

page 96: Dean Martin and some of his bodyguard, the Slaygirls, in *The Ambushers*: *The Ambushers* © 1967, renewed 1995 Columbia Pictures Industries, Inc. All Rights Reserved. Courtesy of Columbia Pictures.

page 102: A scene with Dean Martin in *The Ambushers*: *The Ambushers* © 1967, renewed 1995 Columbia Pictures Industries, Inc. All Rights Reserved. Courtesy of Columbia Pictures.

page 149: Audrey Hepburn and Connie Wald: Wald family photograph.

page 167: Bernie Casey: Bill Ray / Getty Images.

page 186: Joan Didion and John Gregory Dunne: Joan Didion and John Dunne photographed by Jill Krementz on March 31, 1972, at home in Trancas, California.

page 199: Mike Nichols and his wife, Annabel Davis-Goff, and Richard Avedon: Ron Galella / Getty Images.

page 227: Buck Henry and Mike Nichols: © Mary Ellen Mark.